VERMONT FIRSTS

AND OTHER CLAIMS TO FAME

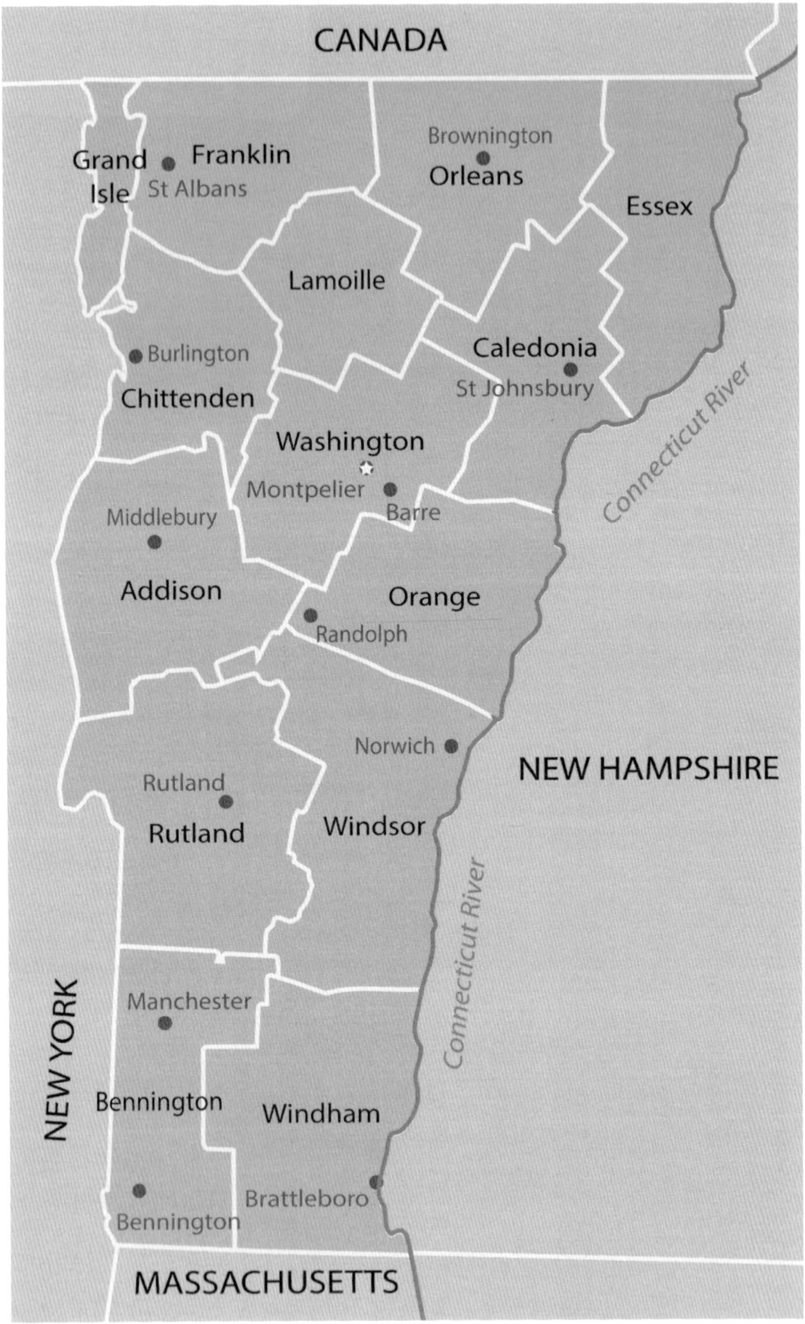

A Vermont map showing the fourteen counties and key towns. Caledonia, Essex and Orleans Counties are considered the Northeast Kingdom. *Courtesy of Spectrum Design.*

VERMONT FIRSTS

AND OTHER CLAIMS TO FAME

Richard B. Smith

THE History PRESS

Published by The History Press
Charleston, SC
www.historypress.com

Front cover, clockwise from top left: Morgan horse UVM Zachariah and Kimberly Demars. *Author's collection*; First Scoutmaster William F. Milne (*right*). *Barre Boy Scout Collection (BHC 11) Barre History Collection, Vermont Historical Society, Barre*; Landmark College. *Landmark College*; First Lady Grace Coolidge with pet raccoon, Rebecca. *Library of Congress*.
Back cover, top to bottom: Bellows Falls Canal. *Library of Congress*; U.S. commemorative stamp honoring the Camp Fire Girls. *Author's collection*; Dorset marble quarry in the early 1900s. *Dorset Historical Society*.

First published 2020

Manufactured in the United States

ISBN 9781467146197

Library of Congress Control Number: 2020938469

CONTENTS

Contents

ACKNOWLEDGEMENTS

Even with modern computer search browsers, it is the help of many people that makes writing a book possible. People at historical societies, other history buffs, nonprofits and a myriad of others have generously given up some of their time to help. Many of the people who helped I have not met in person. Either by phone or email, they have unselfishly provided information or steered me in the right direction. Obtaining images requires finding the right image to tell the story, making sure it is of the correct resolution and determining it has no copyright issues.

The Vermont Historical Society's Leahy Library in Barre has proven invaluable. Librarian Paul Carnahan and Assistant Librarian Marjorie Strong have been of great help in finding files and collections as well as images. Public Program Manager Amanda Gustin was also helpful with her extensive knowledge of Morgan horses.

Peg Pearl at the St. Johnsbury History & Heritage Center and Jennie Shurleff at the Woodstock History Center were very helpful. Molly Veysey at the Orleans County Historical Society provided information of value. Jon Mathewson at the Dorset Historical Society and Museum provided images and information on Dorset quarries.

At the state level, Prudence Doherty at the University of Vermont and Mariessa Dobrick at the Vermont State Archives and Records Administration supplied research information and provided images.

Gail Weiss, Norwich University archivist for digital collections and access services, provided images.

Mary Jane MacGuire at Landmark College along with Todd Miller and Mark DiPietro provided several images and information.

Other nonprofit organizations helped with specific areas of research. Dan Caswell provided information on covered bridges. Ed Homsey provided information and images about Walter Travis. Glenn Estus of the Vermont Philatelic Society was helpful about various commemorative stamps. Victoria Nenno of the USGA provided images and information. Sue Higby of Studio Place Arts provided information and images. Tom Bivens at the Vermont Dairy Industry Association provided some good information on cheese and cheesemakers. Callie Raspuzzi at the Bennington Museum was helpful with images and information.

The Vermont library system has been very helpful with interlibrary loans. The Manchester Community Library has been used frequently, and the Vermont State Library in Barre supplied many books.

Individuals also helped. Perez Ehrich steered me in the right direction with the Vermont Symphony Orchestra. Steve Restelli was all things Scouting. Frank Bryan helped with the Green Mountain Parkway. Peter Prvulovic and Fabio Rossi were helpful with quarry images. John O'Connor helped with some image formatting. Jonah Spivak at Spectrum Design was also helpful. Bill Halligan provided firsthand information about Pearl S. Buck. Kimberly Demars at the UVM Morgan Horse Farm was helpful. Most of all, my wife, Sharon O'Connor, provided advice and took the time to read the manuscript.

INTRODUCTION

As a lover of Vermont history, I have always been fascinated with the fact that so many firsts and other claims to fame in the United States originated in Vermont, which is such a small state. Vermont currently has the second-smallest population in the United States, and it has always had a small population. Historically, the state has been rural, not urban, without large sophisticated cultural centers like Boston, New York and Philadelphia. Even today, 98.3 percent of Vermont is rural land. The land is hilly and rocky, which lends itself to mainly just grazing. Agricultural farming was particularly difficult due to the rocky soil. There is no direct access to the ocean for shipping and commerce to thrive. This book tries to determine why the Vermont settlers and their descendants produced so many claims to fame, despite apparent obstacles.

Definitions are important in identifying some of these claims to fame. For the purposes of this book, *oldest* means the entity, such as a company, hiking trail or golf course, still exists. For instance, the first commercial ski rope tow was in Woodstock. It no longer exists; therefore, it was not designated as the oldest. Designating something as the oldest does not necessarily mean that it was first. For instance, the Green Mountain Club refers to the Long Trail as the oldest, not the first, long-distance hiking trail. No one can say for certain that Native Americans did not have long-distance hiking trails as they traveled around the continent centuries ago. It is possible that cement highways now cover those trails.

Definitions are also important for analyzing competing claims of a first. Many times, different definitions of a term are used. Therefore, in some cases, everyone is correct. For instance, where was the first canal located? A canal can be defined as a ditch, a sluiceway or raceway; therefore, the answer depends on how the term *canal* is described.

A *Vermont claim* must be made by a person who was either born, lived or is buried in Vermont. Sometimes a person moved away after living here or being educated here, but his or her claim to fame was considered a Vermont claim for purposes of this book. If the values and experiences were formed while living in Vermont and these led to his or her particular accomplishments, it was considered a Vermont claim. I attempted giving a qualifying background of each claim to fame, rather than simply listing it.

Many broad commercial claims are almost impossible to prove; therefore, they were not included. For example, it is hard to prove the claim of the "World's Best Ham Sandwich." In addition, only verifiable claims in the United States are included, unless noted otherwise.

Any first or other claim to fame not in the chapter or section title is highlighted in small caps such as FIRST. Sometimes a quote contains the claim first, last, oldest and so forth. That claim is highlighted with small caps, but it was not highlighted in the original quote.

Unless otherwise specified, the claims refer to the United States.

I

FOUNDING OF VERMONT

1

FIRST VICTORY

CAPTURE OF FORT TICONDEROGA, 1775

The first major first that can be attributed to Vermont is the capture of Fort Ticonderoga by Ethan Allen. Other firsts followed shortly after, including firsts in the Vermont Constitution and becoming the first state after the original thirteen states. Who are the people who would accomplish these feats? To understand why these events happened in Vermont, it is necessary to understand the historical context of the type of settlers who came to the area now known as Vermont.

Prior to 1749, the area that is now Vermont was a vast wasteland claimed by New York with essentially no European settlers. In 1749, New Hampshire's Benning Wentworth—through a broad interpretation of his charter from the king of England—claimed that he could charter towns west of the Connecticut River to twenty miles east of the Hudson River. Essentially, that is the area of modern-day Vermont. He proceeded to charter Bennington in 1749 as the first New Hampshire town west of the Connecticut River.

Wentworth chartered a few more towns, but he stopped when the French and Indian War broke out in 1755. By 1760, it was obvious that the British were going to defeat the French. In that year, the area that is now Vermont became safe for English settlers from the coastal colonies to settle. Between 1760 and 1770, New Hampshire's Bennington Wentworth chartered over more than 110 towns in what is Vermont today. Wentworth was offering his New Hampshire land titles in small parcels and at extremely cheap prices. Therefore, many settlers, particularly from Connecticut and Massachusetts, poured into what was called the Northern Frontier; this frontier became known as the New Hampshire Grants. These pioneers were seeking a new life with land they could work themselves and religious freedom.

As the 1760s progressed with more settlers moving to the New Hampshire Grants for cheap land and a better life, the New York governor vehemently objected. New Hampshire–chartered towns were no longer "paper towns." They had real settlers on what the New York governor thought was his land. Towns chartered by New Hampshire overlapped towns chartered by New York. One of the many settlers who came to the New Hampshire Grants from Connecticut was Ethan Allen.

Ethan Allen was born in Litchfield, Connecticut, in 1738. He had been going to what is now Vermont to hunt and trap in the wilderness for many years. Around 1769, he moved to Bennington from Connecticut, where many members of his family still lived. A year later, at age thirty-two, he was asked by the settlers to defend their New Hampshire titles against the New York governor, who claimed the land was owned by New York. Initially, the defense was to be some 1770 trials in Albany to determine whose titles were valid, New York or New Hampshire. After the New York judge ruled that the land was in fact owned by New York, Ethan Allen formed the Green Mountain Boys (GMB) in Bennington to defend with force the New Hampshire title owners against the New York governor and his sheriffs. Allen knew the New York sheriffs would be coming to the New Hampshire Grants to force settlers to pay again for the same land they had purchased from New Hampshire. These settlers had bought land from a legitimate royal governor in New Hampshire and, after clearing the land, were not going to let New York take it away from them.

For five years, from 1771 to 1775, the Green Mountain Boys became a paramilitary group that forcefully held off the New York sheriffs. During this same period, in Boston, tensions between the colonists and England were growing over British taxation and control. These tensions finally broke out into open rebellion on April 19, 1775, with the colonists attacking the British regular army at Lexington and Concord, Massachusetts, and on their return to Boston. The colonists, who needed cannon to drive the British from Boston Harbor, knew there were over seventy-five cannons of various types and sizes at the British-held Fort Ticonderoga in New York on the western shore of Lake Champlain.

Knowing that the Green Mountain Boys had become a strong organized paramilitary militia, a small group of Patriots from Hartford, Connecticut, went to Bennington's Catamount Tavern to ask Ethan Allen to muster his Green Mountain Boys to capture the massive Fort Ticonderoga.

These Green Mountain Boys had come to the New Hampshire Grants for cheap land that they could own and work themselves. They were independent and wanted freedom. They were the

> *most active and rebellious race on the continent,*

as British general John Burgoyne noted two years later. Clearing land without mechanized equipment had been backbreaking work. These settlers were willing to work hard to get a better life. New York represented tyranny. Ethan Allen had more and more been feeling that the New York governor was the king's New York governor. Allen jumped at the opportunity to capture the king's fort.

From Bennington, on May 5, 1775, Ethan Allen marched north, recruiting Green Mountain Boys as he went. He traveled on what is now historic Route 7A to Manchester and then proceeded east on what is now Route 30 to Castleton. From Castleton, he went to Hands Cove on the eastern shore of Lake Champlain. From just a handful of Green Mountain Boys in Bennington, Allen now had over 150 Green Mountain Boys huddled in Hands Cove ready to cross Lake Champlain.

A modern view of Fort Ticonderoga, New York, on Lake Champlain. *Photo by Nathan Farb, courtesy of Fort Ticonderoga.*

The task of capturing Fort Ticonderoga seemed almost impossible to the Green Mountain Boys. They had no artillery, no climbing ladders to go over forty-foot walls, no knowledge of whether the fort had been warned or reinforced. In addition, many of the Green Mountain Boys knew if they were caught, they could be executed by New York authorities.

With only enough boats to take eighty-three men across Lake Champlain, Allen did not want to lose the element of surprise by waiting for more men, so he attacked with just those eighty-three. On May 10, 1775, three weeks after Lexington and Concord, Ethan Allen and his Green Mountain Boys captured the mighty Fort Ticonderoga for America's first victory. Because it was a complete surprise, there was no battle. It was over in less than fifteen minutes. The mighty "Gibraltar of North America," with over seventy-five cannons, was now in America's hands.

Among other accolades, this event has been memorialized with a postage stamp and the naming of a nuclear submarine, USS *Ethan Allen*. Victory is usually associated with holding land, and the colonists held Fort Ticonderoga for the next two years of the Revolution.

2

FIRSTS IN 1777 VERMONT CONSTITUTION

In 1777, two years after Ethan Allen captured Fort Ticonderoga, the American Revolution was still raging. Regardless, settlers in the New Hampshire Grants, through their representatives, formally declared their independence on January 15, 1777, and then ratified a constitution on July 8, 1777, becoming an independent Vermont. There were four significant firsts in that constitution.

First to Have Universal Male Suffrage

Vermont's 1777 constitution was the first in the country to provide for universal male suffrage. This was significant at the time because in many states only a small number of males controlled the government.

For instance, in the 1788–89 election, George Washington was voted in by 43,782 people out of a population of 3 million. Less than 1.8 percent directly participated in the election of the first president. Even in states that voted directly for president, there were many state restrictions on males voting.

Why did Vermont incorporate universal male suffrage into its constitution? Settlers in Vermont had come from states where many males could not vote because of class-based obstacles such as requiring land ownership or certain income levels. Religion was a restriction in Massachusetts and Connecticut. These settlers did not want to be prevented from participating in the political system.

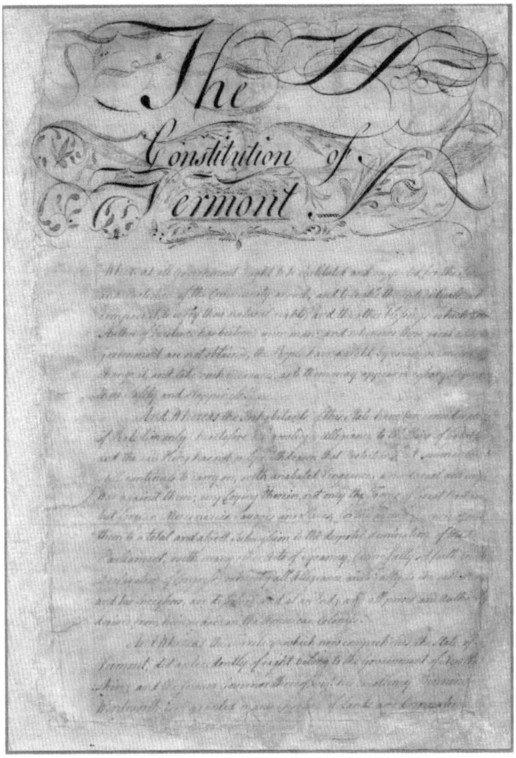
The Constitution of Vermont

Left: The first page of the Vermont Constitution that was signed on July 8, 1777, in Windsor. *Vermont State Archives and Records Administration.*

Below: The Constitution House in Windsor shown in its current location. *Author's collection.*

The settlers had fought New York so fiercely because, in part, they did not want the elitist system practiced by New York. The Dutch-based New York system had large landowners with people working farms rather than individual landowners. Many New York farmers were restricted in their voting because they weren't landowners. Vermont settlers did not have an elite class—nor did they want one.

In the years leading up to outbreak of the Revolution in 1775 and in the two years before 1777, settlers in Vermont (at the time called the New Hampshire Grants) had witnessed abuses by the British and the overpowering New York colony. Many statements in the Vermont Constitution's preamble reflect views to protect against these abuses.

FIRST TO PROVIDE FOR FREE PUBLIC EDUCATION

The constitution of 1777 was adopted in Windsor, about twenty miles south of Norwich, on July 8, 1777. It was the first to provide for a system of public education. A clear system of education was outlined in the constitution: the common school for the towns, grammar schools for the counties and universities for the state. As the federal WPA guide to Vermont states, Vermont was the first state to constitutionally guarantee "a clearly articulated system of education beginning with primary schools and concluding with a university." The exact wording in the 1777 constitution is:

> *Section XL:*
> *A school or schools shall be established in each town, by the legislature, for the convenient instruction of youth, with such salaries to the masters, paid by each town, making proper use of school lands in each town, thereby to enable them to instruct youth at low prices. One grammar school in each county, and one university in this State, ought to be established by direction of the General Assembly.*

Since many documents from 1777 have been lost, it is not clear exactly why Vermont emphasized education. However, the constitutional convention consisted of men from Connecticut and Massachusetts, so they probably incorporated some of these states' practices into the Vermont Constitution. Massachusetts had some town schools, and there were counties in Connecticut that had grammar schools. The mention of "school lands" refers primarily to the town charters from New Hampshire's Benning Wentworth, which set aside school lands for each new town.

Village Schools

The basic schools established under the 1777 constitution rarely went above what is now considered the tenth grade. These schools were to satisfy farmers and others who had come to Vermont for a better life.

County Grammar Schools

Grammar schools gave instruction in college-preparatory subjects and were sometimes referred to as halls, academies, seminaries or institutes. These grammar schools were very similar to what today we refer to as high schools. This constitutional requirement was not implemented immediately because the legislature was slowly splitting old counties into new counties. In 1785, the first public grammar school, Windsor County Grammar School, was chartered by Vermont in Norwich. The second grammar school was chartered in Castleton in 1787 as the Rutland County Grammar School. The funding mechanisms for these and future grammar schools evolved over time. Clio Hall in Bennington was incorporated as a private academy in 1780.

Universities

To implement the 1777 constitution proviso establishing a state university would have been expensive in the late 1770s and early 1780s. In 1786, the Vermont Constitution was changed, and the words "and one university in this state" were dropped.

From 1777 to 1786, there was no official state-funded university. However, during this period of independence, several New Hampshire towns east of the Connecticut River joined the Republic of Vermont, which briefly became Greater Vermont in the early 1780s. One of the New Hampshire towns that became part of Vermont was Dresden (now Hanover). It was the home of Dartmouth College, which was already flourishing; therefore, it became Vermont's unofficial state university. George Washington pressured Vermont to return the New Hampshire towns to New Hampshire, so there was neither a Vermont state university nor a requirement to have one when Vermont joined the union in 1791.

As a side note on Dartmouth, New Hampshire would not give Dartmouth all the funding it needed, so in 1785, Vermont's legislature granted Dartmouth College twenty-three thousand acres in Vermont, thereby being the FIRST state to come to the relief of an educational institution outside its own borders. To fill the void of no university, Ira Allen, who had wanted to make Burlington a cultural center, donated land in 1791 to start a university. This institution evolved into the public University of Vermont.

Several county grammar schools that grew out of the 1777 constitution evolved into universities: Rutland County Grammar School became Castleton University, Orange County Grammar School became Vermont Technical College and the Addison County Grammar School became Middlebury College.

Education System Firsts Continued after the 1777 Constitution

In the 1960s, the Dresden School District, which includes Hanover, New Hampshire, was the FIRST U.S. cross-state (interstate) school district. It was formed under a bill signed by John F. Kennedy in the early 1960s.

The table in the Vermont Constitution House where the Vermont Constitution was signed with all its "firsts." *Author's collection.*

FIRST STATE TO BAN SLAVERY

The Convention of 1777 in Windsor, which ratified the Vermont Constitution on July 8, 1777, inserted the following wording in the constitution:

> *Chapter I A I states simply "therefore, no male person, born in this country, or brought from over sea, ought to be holden by law, to serve any person, as a servant, slave or apprentice after he arrives to the age of twenty-one years, nor female, in like manner, after she arrives to the age of eighteen years"*

Although this wording created only a partial ban on slavery, the Vermont Constitution became the first legislative action to ban any slavery.

Why was Vermont the first state to have a ban on slavery? Since many of the documents from the constitutional convention have been lost, there is only pure speculation about why the representatives inserted this wording. However, putting the status of slavery in context in 1777 may help explain the rationale.

The only other place that the Vermont Constitution made reference to slaves was in the preamble, which reads that the king uses "savages and slaves." In July 1777, while the convention was deliberating, British General Burgoyne and over eight thousand troops were moving south down Lake Champlain toward Saratoga and had captured Fort Ticonderoga. There was a fierce dislike of the king. Expediency may have prompted the convention to ban slaves because the unpopular king was using them.

In general, the settlers from other New England states did not have slaves. Amani Whitfield's well-researched book *The Problem with Slavery in Early Vermont* contains an estimate of 25 black persons in Vermont in around 1770 rising to 270 in 1791, when Vermont became a state. In 1780, just after the constitution was ratified, it was estimated there were 50 African Americans in Vermont. From the early colonial era to statehood, 65 to 70 slaves in Vermont were spread over many towns, with an estimated 30 slave owners. The northern climate meant slaves became a burden during the long winters when farmers were not getting any income. By contrast, around 1775, Connecticut had over an estimated 6,000 slaves. By 1756, New York had an estimated 13,000 slaves. Vermont, therefore, did not have the deep vested interests in slavery because the institution was not an important part of the economic life of the state. The settlers were poor and did not have the ready cash to purchase slaves. There were not wild fears of racial intermixture as in some other states.

The wording banning slavery follows immediately after a declaration of natural rights: "That all men are born equally free and independent, and have certain natural, inherent and unalienable rights."

Slavery was inconsistent with these statements about these rights for all men. To varying degrees, there may have been other reasons for Vermont to ban slavery. The mere incorporation of the passage in the constitution, of course, did not end the practice of slavery in Vermont. Whitfield notes only two slaves in Vermont in 1810. The direction was positive, and other northern states banned slavery shortly after Vermont.

FIRST TO REQUIRE COMPENSATION FOR PROPERTY TAKEN FOR THE PUBLIC GOOD

This requirement became extremely important in the later writing of the U.S. Constitution's Bill of Rights. The Fifth Amendment, regarding eminent domain, has three key words: "without just compensation." Like other parts of the Vermont Constitution, it is not clear exactly why this clause was added. July 8, 1777, was in the middle of the Revolution, so there was mistrust of the British, who did arbitrarily quarter troops in residents' houses. There was, of course, also mistrust of New York, which did not recognize the new independent Vermont. Those hardworking settlers who came to Vermont wanted freedom, and there is essentially no freedom if a government can take property from a person.

3

FIRST STATE AFTER ORIGINAL THIRTEEN STATES TO JOIN UNITED STATES, 1791

For the first six years of Vermont's independence from 1777 to 1783, the United States was still at war with Britain. During that time, thousands of British troops were on the east side of Vermont, the Battle of Bennington was fought, British raiding from Canada attacked Vermont settlers and Britain threatened invasion if independent Vermont didn't become a colony of Great Britain or Canada.

With all the turmoil of the first six years of independence, Vermont emerged after the Revolution essentially economically sound. It had little to no state debts, and since it was not a part of the United States, it did not have any responsibility for national debt. So independent and so successful, Vermont became the first local American government to authorize a private mint to produce coins. The Harmon copper cents were minted in Rupert. The 1785–86 Vermont "coppers," as they were called, had the inscription "Vermontis. Res. Publica," which has been interpreted as being Latin for "Republic of Vermont."

Some coins had been previously in use elsewhere, but they were more like tokens and many were not copper. Most importantly, these other coins didn't have state legislature authority, as they were produced by private minters.

As a further indication of independence, Vermont established its own postal system and provided for a court system in each county. Vermont implemented its own education system and had its own militia, the Green Mountain Boys. So successful was the independent Vermont that several New York and New Hampshire towns joined Vermont to create a "Greater

The original fifteen-stripe, fifteen-star American flag that flew over Fort McHenry in the War of 1812. Vermont's star and stripe were the fourteenth added. The only U.S. flag with fifteen stripes. *Library of Congress.*

Vermont." The population of Vermont went from about twenty thousand in 1776 to around eighty-five thousand in 1791.

During the fourteen years of Vermont's independence, there was instability in the United States. The thirteen U.S. states struggled to pay war debts via taxing as they tried to define the role of the federal government.

People who wanted a better life flocked to independent Vermont. Rebellious farmers like Massachusetts's Daniel Shays and his followers actually fled to the safety of Vermont to escape authorities.

In general, Vermont wanted to become a state and made overtures about becoming a state to the U.S. Congress. However, powerful New York did not recognize Vermont and had resisted statehood for Vermont but eventually relented. Two key factors were involved in New York's relenting to allow Vermont to enter the Union:

- New York's large landowners had claims for the thousands of acres in the so-called Vermont. Vermont paid $30,000 to settle these claims.
- Kentucky had applied for statehood and would be admitted as a slave state. Kentucky would get two votes in the U.S. Senate, reducing the power of New York, but Vermont would be a northern state that would equalize the two Kentucky votes.

Hence, with New York's blessing, on March 4, 1791, Vermont became the fourteenth state. Ratification of the U.S. Constitution took place in Old Bennington on the same green where seven hundred prisoners were brought in 1777 after the Battle of Bennington.

The United States decided to wait until Kentucky entered before changing the flag. The U.S. flag was changed on May 1, 1795, with the addition of two stars and two stripes. That flag would last another twenty-three years. That flag was the same one flown at Fort McHenry during the War of 1812 when Francis Scott Key wrote "The Star-Spangled Banner." The original fifteen-stripe flag is displayed in Washington, D.C.'s Smithsonian National Museum of American History. That flag became the ONLY American flag with more than thirteen stripes. When the sixteenth state joined the union, the U.S. flag went back to thirteen stripes and just a star was added.

Only three states were independent republics immediately before they became a state: Texas for ten years, California for around thirty days and Vermont for fourteen years. Vermont was independent for the LONGEST period and was the FIRST of the three republics to become a state. Hawaii was a territory just before it became a state.

II

LANDSCAPE

4

FIRST IN CONTINENTAL UNITED STATES TO BAN BILLBOARDS

The legislation on outdoor advertising, Act 333, was approved in 1968. Vermont's statute was comprehensive in that both "on-premise" and "off-premise" advertising were extensively covered. The ban covered not just traditional, stand-alone billboards but other forms of outdoor advertising such as barn-side advertisements. The comprehensive statute covered visibility from almost any road the public traveled on, not just state or federal roads.

Why did Vermont pass this legislation? As early as the 1930s, the growing recreation business was bringing more tourists to Vermont. This growth also brought national companies that put up a variety billboards. Opposition to billboards grew. The Rotary Club, the Daughters of the American Revolution and other groups were opposing these monstrosities that were spoiling Vermont's landscape. The Town of Springfield had some billboards removed. In the late 1930s, Vermont's legislature actually passed a statute limiting the use of billboards. Then skiing started to grow in the 1940s, bringing more visitors and more billboards. Then in the early 1960s, the interstates in Vermont were finished, and the same dynamics continued: more tourists and more billboards. Some limitations on billboards had been part of the 1965 Federal Highway Beautification Act, which brought further awareness to the issue.

Conversely, there were pressures to allow billboards because farmers and other landowners were making money by allowing billboards on their land. Businesses liked outdoor advertising, as it brought them customers and created employment—or so they said.

Billboards were removed as part of the 1968 legislation banning billboards and other outdoor advertising. *Vermont State Archives and Records Administration.*

Ted Riehle, a Republican, began promoting anti-billboard legislation to garden groups and anyone who would listen. The legislation passed the legislature and Democratic governor Philip Hoff signed it into law. The bland black-and-white signs giving directions to a place of business do not have logos and are considered information signs.

Currently, there are two states in the continental United States that ban outdoor advertising in some way: Vermont (1968) and Maine (1970s). Alaska banned outdoor advertising in 1998. In the 1920s, Hawaii, which was a territory at the time, put a ban on most billboards. Vermont's outdoor advertising bans were statewide and were arguably more comprehensive by having restrictions not present in the Hawaii statutes. Definitions aside, Vermont was certainly the first state in the continental United States to pass comprehensive statewide, anti–outdoor advertising legislation.

5

MORE AUTHENTIC COVERED BRIDGES PER SQUARE MILE

This *most* refers to authentic covered bridges as defined by the Federal Highway Administration: "covered bridges supported by longitudinal trusses built of relatively large (heavy) timber components." In other words, the truss walls of the bridge support the roadway. A covered bridge with the roadway supported by steel or timber beams (stringers) underneath the roadway that go in the same direction as the roadway is not an authentic covered bridge. There is a roof covering the roadway, and in some cases, the side trusses are covered.

The United States has fewer than 900 authentic covered bridges still standing. Vermont has 101 authentic bridges, according to the National Society for the Preservation of Covered Bridges. Pennsylvania has the most with 213, with Ohio second with 148. However, Vermont has 9,250 square miles, Pennsylvania 44,817 square miles and Ohio 40,948 square miles. Vermont, therefore, by far, has more authentic covered bridges per square mile than these states and any other state. For example,

Authentic Covered Bridges Per 1,000 Square Miles	
Vermont	10.9
Pennsylvania	4.8
Ohio	3.6

Given the size of Vermont and the topography, this means the probability of using, seeing and enjoying an authentic covered bridge on a

This is an authentic covered bridge. It is in West Arlington near Normal Rockwell's former home and studio. Notice truss supports on the side walls. *Author's collection.*

trip to Vermont is higher than any other state. Also, the covered bridges in Vermont tend to be clustered together, which makes them more convenient to view and use.

The most accepted reason for why there is a roof and/or covered sides is that the covered parts of the bridge protect the wood from getting wet and then rotting. Other reasons for having a roof include protecting the floor from getting wet and freezing, thereby preventing horse-drawn carriages from sliding into the river. Being a northern state, there were pressures to build these bridges to protect the wood from the harsh winters and weather in Vermont.

Not only is Vermont first on the list of authentic covered bridges per square mile but it also has the longest historic covered bridge. The Windsor-Cornish Bridge spans the Connecticut River between Vermont and New Hampshire. If you measure the truss of the Windsor-Cornish Bridge, the span is 449.5 feet, versus 434 feet for the shorter truss of the Medora Bridge in Indiana. However, if you measure the span from the abutments, the Medora Bridge span is 430.4 feet, and the Windsor-Cornish Bridge span is 422 feet. Take your pick on definition. There is a covered bridge in Ohio that is 613 feet long, but it was built in 2008; therefore, it is not considered historic.

The Windsor-Cornish Bridge spans the Connecticut River. The U.S. Supreme Court ruled that the western bank, not the middle of the Connecticut River, is the border with New Hampshire. This means that the Windsor-Cornish Bridge is almost entirely in New Hampshire. However, to cross the bridge you have to touch Vermont. Some covered bridge groups count the bridge as being in both Vermont and New Hampshire. There are 3 covered bridges over the Connecticut River; therefore, if they are counted for just New Hampshire, Vermont has 98 authentic covered bridges, not the 101 previously mentioned.

The National Society for the Preservation of Covered Bridges has extensive detailed lists of the covered bridges in each state by county. If nonauthentic bridges are included, Vermont has more than another seventy-five covered bridges. In some cases, the type is not known because they are private and hidden from the road.

6
ONLY STATE CAPITAL WITHOUT A McDONALD'S RESTAURANT

If there is a list of capitals with the number of McDonald's in ascending order, Montpelier is the first, with none. This unique claim goes back decades. Over two decades ago, in the 1990s, Vermont was promoting and acknowledging that its state capital did not have a McDonald's, as shown on the promotional cup in the image.

Montpelier is also the SMALLEST U.S. state capital, with a 2019 population estimate of 7,500 people. The next smallest is Pierre, South Dakota, with about 14,000. Montpelier's small size adds to its charm.

A 1990s coffee cup claiming Montpelier is the only state capital (the capit*o*l is a building or buildings) without a McDonald's. *Author's collection.*

7

ONLY STATE TO BE SELECTED AS A WORLD'S GREATEST DESTINATION

In celebration of the turn of the century, in October 1999, *National Geographic Traveler* published a special collection issue. This magazine identified the top fifty "World's Greatest Destinations." These fifty "places of a lifetime" included some of the world's most famous wonders such as the Taj Mahal in India and the Great Wall in China. Of the fifty destinations, only six were in the continental United States and only one was an entire state:

Big Sur (California)
Grand Canyon (Arizona)
Mesa Verde (Colorado)
New York City (New York)
San Francisco (California)
Vermont (Vermont)

The Hawaiian "Islands" were listed but not the State of Hawaii in the original fifty destinations. It was not clear why the reference was to the islands and not the state. However, the islands of the State of Hawaii are only 58.75 percent of the total area of the state.

Vermonter Noel Perrin (since deceased) wrote the Vermont section of this special issue and gives an interesting summary of why the entire state was selected. Remembering the rural reputation of Vermont, he quotes from *Moby-Dick*, "Ah, poor hay seed," said with contempt of a Vermonter looking

The entire state of Vermont: One of *National Geographic Traveler*'s fifty "places of a lifetime" to visit in the world. *Author's collection.*

for work in New Bedford, Massachusetts. The laugh is now on the other foot. Vermont is now a great place live and to visit.

Why the entire state of Vermont? According to Perrin, it lacks urban blight. The rural nature has not led to explosive population growth. *Poverty* was the key word for a century between 1840 and 1940. Poverty became a plus. Without money, old buildings were saved and restored, not razed.

Perrin also credits the 1968 Vermont statewide legislation (Act 333) with its ban on billboards for making Vermont free of the gaudy signs many other states have. Vermont is so serious about billboards, Perrin asserted that if there is no removal of some signs, owners have to pay an "uglification" fine.

Perrin also credits glaciers, politicians and cows for placing Vermont as one of the fifty destinations of a lifetime. Thanks to glaciers twelve thousand years ago, we have a multitude of micro-regions, creating many different scenic delights. Vermont's politicians, mostly non-lawyers, protected the Vermont landscape with Act 250, which controls and protects Vermont's scenic hills and valleys statewide. Cows grazing in the fields are a personification of harmony, tranquility and beauty.

III

MILITARY

8

YOUNGEST MEDAL OF HONOR RECIPIENT

William "Willie" H. Johnston was born in 1850 in Morristown, New York. His family moved and landed in Montreal before moving again in 1859 to Salem (which became part of Derby) in Orleans County. Derby is on the Vermont/Canada border in the Northeast Kingdom about ten miles from Brownington.

In 1861, when the Civil War broke out, Willie's father enlisted in the Union army. Not wanting to be left behind without his father, Willie, at age eleven, was allowed to join the army as a drummer boy in D Company of the Third Vermont Volunteer Infantry Regiment. Before heading south, he mustered at St. Johnsbury, also in the Northeast Kingdom.

In 1862, General George McClellan's Army of the Potomac began the massive and famous Peninsula Campaign, which included an amphibious landing in Virginia and then a march northwest with the intent of capturing Richmond, the capital of the Confederacy.

Initially, the campaign was successful. However, the Confederate general Robert E. Lee drove the Union army back from its advance on Richmond. During the Union retreat, there were several battles between June 25 and July 1, 1862, later known as the Seven Days Battles. As Lee advanced south, many retreating Union army troops dropped their equipment to retreat faster. Musicians did the same, dropping their instruments.

Of all the musicians, Willie Johnston did not drop his drum and returned after the battles with his drum in working order. Drummers were used in

Willie Johnston, Civil War drummer, youngest Medal of Honor recipient. *St. Johnsbury History and Heritage Center.*

the Civil War to muster troops, communicate and instill pride. Willie then played for the whole division. He was eleven years old.

When President Abraham Lincoln heard of this bravery, he recommended Willie for the Medal of Honor. On September 16, 1863, Edward Stanton, the Union war secretary, bestowed Willie with the Medal of Honor. At that time, he was thirteen years old. He remains the youngest Medal of Honor winner in U.S. history.

It should be noted that the Medal of Honor had just been created about the time of the Seven Days Battles. Also, at the time, the only other medal that could have been awarded was the Purple Heart.

9

LARGEST FAMILY MORTALITY IN THE CIVIL WAR

Brian Knight, in his thoroughly researched book *No Braver Deeds*, gives a stirring account of the Battle of Savage Station in Virginia on June 29, 1862. The Cummings family—five brothers (Hiram, Edmund, William, Asabel "Silas" and Henry), a cousin (William H.) and a brother-in-law (Horace Clayton)—was part of Company E of the Fifth Vermont Regiment. They had mustered in St. Albans, Franklin County, prior to going to Virginia.

The Fifth Vermont was part of the Peninsula Campaign, which was designed to land in Southeast Virginia and head northwest to capture Richmond. However, Robert E. Lee fought back and forced a retreat of the Union army. During the retreat, there was a series of encounters known as the Seven Days Battles. One of those battles was at Savage Station, Virginia, on June 29, 1862. The Cummings family was caught in a crossfire and decimated within a few minutes. All were killed or mortally wounded.

In 1897, Warren Dunton of Company E stated, "This is the greatest mortality in any one family in the Union, for either a single battle or during the war." In his excellent 2013 Civil War book about Vermont, *Something Abides*, author Howard Coffin says the Cummings family was the "family that probably suffered the greatest loss sustained by any family, North or South, in the civil war."

As mentioned in the preceding chapter, Vermont's Willie Johnston from Derby, the youngest Medal of Honor recipient, received the award for his valor during the Seven Days Battles. Johnston and his Third Vermont Regiment were also at Savage Station.

10

MOST NORTHERN ACTION IN THE CIVIL WAR

Some say the event in St. Albans was an action, others say it was a raid, even others say it was a battle, and some even say it was just a bank robbery or a confrontation. The noted Vermont Civil War historian Howard Coffin calls it an "action," with the action being a "raid." Whatever the term, there was death.

For several days in mid-October 1864, about twelve Confederate soldiers who had escaped from Union prisons drifted into St. Albans from Canada. Since St. Albans, which is about twenty miles from Canada, was an active train stop, these Confederate soldiers went unnoticed.

On October 19, the Confederates, under their leader, Kentuckian Bennet Young, gathered in one of the hotels to plan an attack on local banks. In early afternoon, they entered three banks brandishing their weapons. Some townspeople were taken as prisoners to Taylor Park and guarded. Within twenty minutes, $208,000 was successfully taken from three banks.

As the Confederates were leaving on stolen horses to return to Canada, the people in St. Albans opened fire and wounded one of the men. Some had actually been in uniform during the robbery. As the Confederates fled, they returned fire and tried to throw firebombs into buildings. During this exchange of gunfire, the Confederates killed a man from New Hampshire, Elnius J. Morrison. One other person was wounded, but Morrison was the only person killed in the raid. A posse

Drawing of the murder of E.J. Morrison during the St. Albans raid. *University of Vermont, Bailey Howe Library Special Collections.*

was formed under George Conger and chased the Confederates to Canada. The Confederates escaped with the money (and horses), making it a Confederate victory.

Many of the sites involved (banks, hotels, park) are still visible today in St. Albans.

11

FIRST AND ONLY ADMIRAL OF THE NAVY

George Dewey was born in Montpelier, the state capital, on December 26, 1837, to physician Julius Dewey and his first wife, Mary Perrin. He was born across the street from the Vermont Statehouse. In 1848, George's father and others founded the National Life Insurance Company, which is still based in Montpelier.

George Dewey's association with the military started when he was fifteen years old. After attending schools in nearby rural Johnson, about forty miles north of Montpelier, he attended Norwich University (then in Norwich) for two years. Immediately after leaving Norwich, Dewey entered the U.S. Naval Academy in 1854. Dewey finished fifth in his small class.

In 1862, the year after the Civil War broke out, Dewey found himself assigned to a frigate as part of David Farragut's Union fleet. The frigate was tasked to clear the Mississippi River for the capture of New Orleans. This was the first operation that clearly distinguished Dewey as an officer. After the Civil War, Dewey had various assignments, including Europe, Newport, Rhode Island's torpedo station, Pacific Coast Survey, lighthouse inspector and a Washington bureau officer.

When the Spanish-American War started in 1896, Dewey was almost sixty years old. Dewey's assignment was to be commander of the Asiatic Squadron. On April 27, 1896, Dewey set sail from Hong Kong to the Spanish-controlled Philippines to attack the Spanish in Manila Bay. On April 30, 1898, Dewey sailed to the mouth of Manila Bay, and the next morning, he gave his famous command: "You may fire when you are ready, Gridley." Dewey defeated

Admiral of the Navy George Dewey. Notice the unique insignia on the epaulets indicating the one-of-a-kind rank. *Library of Congress.*

the Spanish in a battle that lasted about six hours. In that battle, he beat the entire Spanish Pacific squadron either by sinking or capturing enemy ships. Amazingly, Dewey's operation had no loss of life on the American side, although some reports indicate there was one U.S. death.

In May 1898, Dewey was made rear admiral, and in 1899, he was made full admiral. He returned to the United States on September 27, 1899, to a full hero's welcome. There was a two-day parade in New York and a celebration in Washington, with President McKinley giving him a special sword. As a tribute to Dewey, the United States produced the Battle of Manila Bay Medal, which is commonly referred to as the Dewey Medal. Numerous places in America were named after George Dewey, including Dewey Hall at Norwich University. Three navy ships have been named USS *Dewey*, and Dewey Hall and Dewey Field at the U.S. Naval Academy are named after him.

Probably one of Dewey's proudest thanks came from his home state of Vermont when October 12, 1899, was declared Dewey Day in Montpelier. There were special trains from Boston and, of course, parades with daylong celebrations for Montpelier's native son.

In 1903, George Dewey, by an act of Congress, was given the highest naval rank possible, Admiral of the Navy. This title was made retroactive to 1899. Dewey was the first and to date the only American to bear it. George Dewey died fourteen years later at age eighty. His remains are in the Bethlehem Chapel of the Washington National Cathedral.

12

FIRST TO GIVE INTELLIGENCE BEFORE LEXINGTON

Solomon Brown was born on January 15, 1756. As a nineteen-year-old, Brown found himself in a market in Boston on April 18, 1775, and returned home to Lexington on the same day. According to the *Gazetteer and Business Directory of Addison County, Vermont, for 1881–1882*, on returning home, Brown reported to Colonel William Munroe that he "had seen nine British officers, dressed in blue great-coats, passing leisurely along the road, keeping sometimes before and sometimes after him. All were armed." Thus, he was the first person to bring intelligence into Lexington that British officers were going to Lexington.

The next day, April 19, 1775, the colonists fired on the British regulars advancing to Lexington and Concord. The American Revolution was on. Who fired the first effective shot that hit a British regular?

Some accounts have Solomon firing the first shot, but Sergeant William Munroe testified fifty years after the fateful day that Solomon Brown fired from the rear of the Buckman Tavern in Lexington and then from the front. However, Brown's firings occurred after the first shots had been fired. Apparently, Brown didn't wait for orders to shoot.

In 1825, Elias Phinney said it was Brown who was seen taking aim and probably inflicted the wound that hit the British soldier in the Tenth Regiment. There is no record of anyone witnessing the impact, but Elias Phinney did see Brown aim in that direction. Several other people saw blood, and Brown had fired in that direction at the British regulars. Therefore, it is thought that the first effective American shot in the Revolution goes to Solomon Brown.

There are several accounts with good research in *Paul Revere's Ride* by Pulitzer Prize–winning author David Hackett Fischer.

Although born in Lexington, Massachusetts, Solomon Brown at age thirty-one moved to New Haven, about ten miles north of Middlebury. In that year, 1787, Vermont was an independent republic. Brown lived in New Haven another fifty years and died there at age eighty-one in 1837, and he is buried there in Evergreen Cemetery.

IV

EDUCATION

13
FIRST PRIVATE MILITARY COLLEGE

Norwich University, which has many firsts to its credit, was founded by Captain Alden Partridge, who was born on February 12, 1785, on a family farm in Norwich. His father had fought in the Revolutionary War, including the Saratoga battles in 1777. As a youth, Alden used to do considerable hiking and attended nearby Dartmouth College from 1802 to 1805. Subsequently, he attended and then graduated from the U.S. Military Academy (West Point) in 1806. Later, he became the superintendent of West Point.

His novel education philosophy, which he called the "American System of Education," linked military and civilian studies to produce enlightened and useful citizen-soldiers. His philosophy also included rigorous physical training. Since this approach was not well received by Congress, he left West Point at age thirty-four, returned to his childhood home in Norwich and founded the American Literary, Scientific and Military Academy in 1819. This was the first private military college in the United States and would later be named Norwich University. The following year, 1820, a band was organized at the school, making the Norwich band the OLDEST collegiate band in the United States. Later, Norwich University would become the FIRST private institution to teach engineering.

The Partridge philosophy of education included more practical courses, enabling students to become better prepared for life after graduating. In 1834, the State of Vermont gave a charter to the school as Norwich University. A fire in 1866 prompted the school to move to Northfield, about ten miles south of Montpelier.

Norwich University cadets, after the school began voluntarily admitting women as cadets. *Courtesy of Norwich University Archives, Northfield, Vermont.*

The Civil War years produced the Morrill Act of 1862, which established land grant colleges. Justin Morrill lived near Alden Partridge, who was Morrill's senior by about twenty-five years. Although Partridge had died in 1854, before the Morrill Act, they had communicated about having schools both civilian and military. Part of the Morrill Act required land grant schools to include military tactics in their curriculum. As the founder of Norwich, Partridge had promoted the idea of a citizen-soldier who would do civilian work in peacetime and become a soldier in wartime. Norwich became the "Birthplace of ROTC." Ironically, during the 1860s and 1870s, Norwich resisted being a land grant college, although it was actually offering a curriculum similar to the one prescribed in the Morrill Act.

The twentieth century brought more firsts to Norwich University. In 1916, during World War I, the War Department designated Norwich as the FIRST site for a Senior ROTC cavalry unit. In 1974, Norwich became the FIRST private military school in the country to fully and voluntarily integrate women into the Corps of Cadets.

Located on a 1,200-acre campus in rural Northfield, Vermont, Norwich University now has over 2,000 undergraduates and 1,300 postgraduates.

14

FIRST COLLEGE SOLELY FOR STUDENTS WITH LEARNING DISABILITIES

Opened for students in 1985, this Putney, Vermont college has become so successful that in 2020, *U.S. News & World Report* ranked Landmark College the "Best Undergraduate Teaching and Most Innovative College" in the United States and one of the best colleges in the Northeast.

Landmark's Vermont connection goes back much further than 1985. In 1951, in their home, Dr. Walter Hendricks and his wife, Flora, founded the Vermont Institute for Special Studies in Putney. The name was later changed to Windham College. Putney is located in Windham County. In 1961, Windham broke ground for a new campus designed by noted architect Edward Durell Stone. By 1962, the school had about 25 faculty members and 250 students. However, in the late 1970s, Windham College ran into financial problems and closed in 1978. The beautiful campus would sit empty for years.

At about the same time, in the early 1970s, Dr. Charles "Chad" Drake and his wife, Marjorie, founded the Landmark School in Massachusetts to address the needs of students with language-based learning disabilities such as dyslexia. Chad Drake himself was a Harvard-trained educator with dyslexia. As the school expanded from its 1971 founding, Drake and other trustees started to explore the possibility of opening a college specially, specifically and exclusively designed for students with learning disabilities. Drake and others found the perfect site for the new college—the former campus of Windham College with its beautiful 125 acres in Putney, just north of Brattleboro.

Landmark College campus, Putney. *Landmark College.*

Landmark College was established in 1983, and the first 77 students matriculated in September 1985. Although primarily for dyslexia, Landmark has since expanded to help others who learn differently, such as students with Attention Deficit Hyperactivity Disorder (ADHD). Landmark now has about 490 students and offers associate's and bachelor's degrees in disciplines like computing. Through an association with another school, Landmark also offers some graduate certificates. All applicants must show documentation of a condition that significantly impairs learning.

Landmark has truly separated fundamental intelligence from a learning disability. Many famous people reportedly have had dyslexia, including Leonardo Da Vinci, Henry Ford, Alexander Graham Bell and Thomas Edison. If a learning disability is not separated from intelligence, some very talented people might not get into college. Here is a piece written by someone with dyslexia: "Geuins is oue dercent insidiratiou, ninety-nine dercent derspiratiou."

The first reaction of a college admissions officer reviewing this writing on an application might be that this person is not smart and might not accomplish much in his life. The actual quote is: "Genius is one percent inspiration, ninety-nine percent perspiration"—attributed to dyslexic Thomas Alva Edison.

15

FIRST FEDERALLY FUNDED PUBLIC COLLEGES

Justin Morrill was born in Strafford, Orange County, Vermont, on April 14, 1810, died at eighty-eight on December 28, 1898, and is buried in Strafford. His early education was at the Thetford Academy and Randolph Academy in Orange County. Yearning to go to college but unable to afford it, Morrill became a successful self-taught man. He learned business, architecture, horticulture, politics and other disciplines on his own.

After a successful business career as a merchant and investor, Morrill was essentially able to retire from commerce. He entered politics at age forty-four and was elected to the U.S. House of Representatives as a Whig. He became disenchanted with the Whig Party and, along with Jacob Merritt Howard (Shaftsbury), helped found the Republican Party. He served in the House from March 4, 1855, to March 3, 1867, having been elected the last five times as a Republican. In 1866, he was elected as a Vermont senator and served from March 4, 1867, until his death in 1898. He had a remarkable career in Congress spanning forty-three years.

Although he was a successful legislator in Congress, Morrill's major lasting significant legislation was the Morrill Act, also known as the Land Grant College Act of 1862. This was the first federal legislation that provided federal funding for higher education in every state and was designed to help people who normally might not be able to afford college. Truly visionary, the act proposed the establishment of "at least" one college in every state accessible to all, especially to the "sons of toil." The education would be broad, including agriculture and mechanical subjects as well as some

The 1955 U.S. commemorative stamp honoring land grant colleges. *Author's collection.*

military disciplines. It was followed up with a second land grant Morrill Act in 1890. In total, over 105 colleges and universities were supported or founded as a result of these land grant acts. Many famous universities are land grant schools and have a Morrill Hall or other building to recognize the importance of the Morrill Acts.

It was not required that colleges be founded after 1862. If the state designated a school as its land grant school, that school was eligible to receive federal funding from the sale of federal lands and other support. The intent of both land grant Morrill Acts of 1862 and 1890 and the subsequent 1994 Land Grant Act was to make education more accessible to more people.

16

FIRST SCHOOL FOR TEACHERS

Samuel Read Hall was born on October 27, 1795, in Croydon, New Hampshire, near the Vermont border. However, when he was less than a year old, his family moved north to the wilderness of Guildhall in Essex County in the Northeast Kingdom. Educated at home, he never attended college.

Hall moved around considerably before starting the first school for teachers in 1823. In 1818, the twenty-three-year-old studied for the ministry in Meriden, New Hampshire. When he was twenty-eight years old, after finishing teaching assignments in Maine and Massachusetts, he was licensed to preach. He then returned to his first church in Concord about twelve miles east of St. Johnsbury in the Northeast Kingdom.

Hall accepted the Concord position on the condition that he would be able to open a school for educating teachers. In 1823, within a week of arriving in Concord, he opened the first training school for teachers, recognized in the United States as the Concord Academy. In 1829, he published the FIRST American instructional book for teachers; it eventually was reprinted over ten times. The following year, he co-founded the American Institute of Instruction, the OLDEST educational organization in the United States.

After leaving Concord in 1830, he moved to Andover, Massachusetts, becoming principal of Phillips Academy's new program for teacher education (1830–37). He moved again in 1837 to Plymouth, New Hampshire, to serve at the Holmes-Plymouth Academy (1837–40). From 1840 to 1846, he returned to Vermont and taught at the Craftsbury Academy in Orleans

The 1957 U.S. commemorative stamp honoring teachers. *Author's collection.*

County, again in the rural Northeast Kingdom. From the 1823 opening of the Concord Academy until 1839, he was the only professional trainer of teachers in America.

From 1854 to 1867, Hall was pastor of the Brownington Church. He died on June 24, 1877. His Brownington home is part of the beautiful Brownington Historic District. Although he never went to college and spent decades in the vast rural Northeast Kingdom of Vermont, Hall nonetheless is credited with establishing the first school for teachers. He recognized the value and importance of educators.

17

FIRST AFRICAN AMERICAN TO GET A COLLEGE DEGREE

Alexander Twilight was born on September 23, 1795, in rural Corinth, Orange County, Vermont. Only four years prior, Vermont had become the fourteenth state.

Ichabod and Mary Twilight were his parents, and the town history listed them as "the first negroes to settle in Corinth." Little is known about Alexander's parents except that Ichabod served as a "private" in the Continental army from 1782 to 1783. Anything else about Alexander's parents is speculation. There are a lot of "probablys" and "maybes" in Alexander's history.

Records do indicate, however, that Alexander worked on a nearby Corinth farm starting around 1803, when he was eight years old. There is no indication he was working as anything other than a free farmhand. Over the next twelve years, he learned to read, write and do math. In 1815, at age twenty, he enrolled in nearby Randolph's Orange County Grammar School, about thirty miles from Corinth.

In the six years from 1815 to 1821, he completed secondary school and two years of college-level courses. He was accepted to Middlebury College in 1821. Entering as a junior, he graduated in 1823. Middlebury College claims he is the first African American to earn a bachelor's degree from an American college or university.

In 1829, after teaching in New York and Vergennes, Alexander Twilight became principal of the Orleans County Grammar School in Brownington. He was also "acting pastor" of the Congregational Church in Brownington. Upon arrival in Brownington, he moved into a small house a few hundred

Alexander Twilight's Athenian Hall in Brownington. Notice the original granite. *Author's collection.*

yards from his school. He immediately started building a large granite house across the street to accommodate eight to ten boarding students. His school continued to grow rapidly. This building was occupied in 1836 and was called Athenian Hall.

In 1836, Alexander Twilight became the town's state legislator and, in doing so, became the FIRST African American to serve in a U.S. state legislature. Unfortunately, in 1847, squabbles about school finances and other issues forced Twilight to move a short distance away in nearby Canada. The school floundered after he left, but he was then asked to return in 1852. He taught until 1855, when he suffered a stroke and died two years later. He is buried in the Brownington cemetery next to the church where he had been a pastor. His wife is buried next to him.

Athenian Hall in Brownington is open to the public and serves as the Orleans County Historical Society and Museum.

FIRST IN STUDENT PERFORMANCE

Even going into the twenty-first century, education for K–12 students has always been important in Vermont. Education rankings and criteria change from year to year. In 2010, the American Legislative Exchange Council (ALEC) ranked Vermont first on the list of state student performance.

V

QUARRIES

18

FIRST COMMERCIAL MARBLE QUARRY

A Vermont state historical marker states that the quarry in South Dorset was the first marble quarry in the United States, established in 1785. However, it should probably read first "commercial" quarry, but due to space limitations, markers cannot include every word or qualifier. Small local quarries probably existed prior to 1785. The marble Manley house was built around 1773, which is prior to the building of the first commercial quarry next door. Some marble for buildings came from surface ledges rather than pure quarries.

On land owned by Reuben Bloomer, Isaac Underhill began his commercial quarry operations in 1785, shortly after the Revolutionary War ended. It is now known as the Norcross-West quarry because of later owners. A walk around the quarry gives clues as to why this was the first commercial quarry in the United States. The marble vein for this quarry is very close to the surface, with several outcroppings visible today. The entire area is also flat, which meant it would be economical to bring marble out by horse-drawn carriages. In 1785, veins of commercially viable marble had been discovered in Dorset. Some of these veins (strata) went over fifty miles to the north to Rutland and Proctor.

The Dorset quarry was not a short-lived quarrying operation producing only tombstones. This particular quarry led to the development of many other quarries and processing mills in the Dorset area. With the opening of the Lake Champlain Canal in 1819 and the coming of the railroad in the 1850s, marble from the first marble quarry (the Norcross-West quarry as it is

First commercial marble quarry in the early 1900s in Dorset, Vermont. The quarry is now a swimming hole. *Dorset Historical Society*.

known today) was being shipped all over the United States during the 1800s. The marble was being used for high-quality architectural uses far beyond simple sidewalks and headstones.

The Dorset Norcross-West quarry was closed in the late 1800s due to economic reasons. However, in the 1890s, Orlando Norcross, a building contractor from Massachusetts, and local entrepreneur Spafford West formed a partnership to provide the massive marble columns for the New York Public Library. Since then, the first commercial quarry has been called the Norcross-West quarry. On May 1, 1900, construction started on the largest marble building in the world at the time. A thing of beauty, the New York Public Library is a Beaux-Arts masterpiece covering an entire block on Forty-Second Street and Fifth Avenue. A five-mile short-line railroad was built to carry the massive amounts of marble from Dorset to nearby Manchester for processing and trans-shipment to New York. The adjacent Plateau quarry provided the marble for the Daughters of the American Revolution (DAR) Constitution Hall in Washington.

A popular swimming hole now, the quarry is located less than one hundred feet from Route 30 in Dorset and is fully visible from the road. The Dorset Historical Society has a marvelous exhibit with images and information about all the area quarries. It has lists of all the structures, many famous, that use Dorset marble.

19

LARGEST UNDERGROUND MARBLE QUARRY

Although marble is no longer shipped from Dorset's first commercial quarry, the Norcross-West quarry, commercial marble quarrying still continues underground inside the same stratum through an aperture on the northeast side of Dorset Mountain. The highest point in the Dorset Mountain Range is actually located in Danby about a few hundred yards from the Danby-Dorset line. Millions of cubic feet have been extracted from that underground quarry, which is entered through the same opening used over a century ago.

Started in 1903, the Danby quarry has become the largest underground marble quarry in the world, going for one and a half miles into Dorset Mountain. Today, it encompasses about twenty-five acres producing 200,000 cubic feet per year. Marble blocks up to ninety-three tons have been quarried. The quarry produces about ten different types of marble. As another indication of the size of this underground quarry, a full-scale production facility is located inside, where up to 4,000 square feet of slabs per day can be produced. This factory itself is perhaps the largest in the United States or even North America.

This quarry is famous for both its size and high-quality marble, making it ideal for the construction of many famous structures. For instance, the colonnaded façade of the Arlington National Cemetery Amphitheater, dedicated on May 15, 1920, is primarily Danby marble. Washington's Supreme Court building's famous front façade uses Danby Imperial marble. Constructed from 1939 to 1943, the Jefferson Memorial uses

World's largest underground marble quarry in Danby. *Vermont Quarries Inc.*

white Danby marble. The United Nations building in New York City uses Danby marble. On a smaller scale, Martha Stewart used Danby marble for her home.

The Danby quarry is now owned by RED Granti and Mazzucchelli Marmi of Carrara, Italy. It is operated under the name of Vermont Quarries Corporation.

Suggested reading would be Tyler Resch's excellent book *Dorset: In the Shadow of Marble Mountain*. Also, YouTube has some wonderful videos of trips inside the Danby Imperial quarry. (Search the site for "Danby Vermont marble quarry.")

20

LARGEST DEEP-HOLE DIMENSION GRANITE QUARRY

Originally chartered on November 6, 1780, as Wildersburgh, the town was renamed Barre after Isaac Barre of England, who had been friendly to the colonies. About thirty years later, around the time of the War of 1812, the Barre granite industry exploded. Vast amounts of granite were discovered in the Millstone Hill area. More specifically, vast meant, by some estimates, granite deposits four miles long by two miles wide and, most important, ten miles deep. Barre gray granite has a fine grain, even texture and superior weather resistance. The first granite quarry became known as the Wheaton quarry.

The Barre quarry industry continued to grow over the next century. New technologies were introduced, and the railroad, which came to Barre in 1875, opened new markets. With this growth came thousands of immigrants with stone-carving skills, opening even more markets. By 1910, the population of Barre had grown to over twelve thousand from two thousand in 1880. From forty quarries in the 1890s, Barre grew to about sixty-eight producing quarries in 1902 according to the Barre Granite Association.

One of the innovators in the quarry industry was Emery L. Smith, who was born in Northfield in 1842. He attended nearby Orange County Grammar School in Randolph. Through a series of moves, he became a prominent granite processor and owned many quarry facilities at different times. An innovator, E.L. Smith used new technologies of electrically detonated explosives, permanent derricks and steam drills. E.L. Smith became the first mayor of Barre, and his legacy still lives on through one of his quarries.

Largest deep-hole dimension granite quarry, the E.L. Smith quarry. It is located in Barre, Vermont. *Vermont Historical Society, Barre.*

Today, the E.L. Smith quarry, which is part of the Rock of Ages operation, is the world's largest deep-hole dimension granite quarry in the world. It is about six hundred feet deep with water covering part of the depth. *Dimension* means that granite is removed in blocks as opposed to gravel from blasting for products like granular calcium carbonate. The E.L. Smith quarry is one of the last quarries in Barre and is open to the public for viewing.

Barre granite has been used in memorials throughout the world. Locally, beautiful granite monuments are visible throughout Barre in such places as the twenty-five-acre Hope Cemetery.

21

LARGEST MARBLE EXHIBIT IN THE WORLD

Located just outside Rutland in Proctor, the marble museum is located in the former Vermont Marble Company facility. Reportedly, the marble museum is the largest marble exhibit in the world. Although it is hard to define "largest," the building is ninety thousand square feet and the former home of what was the world's LARGEST marble company, the Vermont Marble Company. The museum contains a vast number of photographs, marble sculptures, artifacts and marble history information. In itself, the exhibit is a history of the many immigrant groups that worked in the marble industry in Vermont.

In Barre, there is the Vermont Granite Museum, which is also educational and fascinating. Although the Granite Museum does not claim to be the largest, it is located in the historic Jones Brothers Manufacturing plant and is in the National Register of Historic Places.

VI

SPORTING LIFE

22

OLDEST MAIL-ORDER COMPANY

The Orvis Company, a privately held company, is the oldest mail-order retailer. Not only is it the oldest but it has also become a major mail-order retailer over the last century. Orvis now has mailings of over forty-four million catalogues, which account for over 70 percent of its sales. Orvis has also been called the LONGEST continually operating fly-fishing business.

The Vermont experience and lifestyle explains why Orvis was the first mail-order retailer. Charles F. Orvis was born in 1831 and grew up in and around Manchester. In rural Bennington County, field sports such as fishing and hunting were available everywhere, and Charles loved the outdoors.

A major life event for Charles Orvis was the simple act of watching an experienced fly-fisherman cast and angle. After studying how other rods were made, Orvis started to make his own rods, as a hobby. He was barely in his twenties.

Vermont and Manchester, in particular, were changing in the early 1850s. Tourism was increasing to the point that it was rivaling the importance of the marble processing business. In 1852, the railroad came to Manchester and other Vermont towns, which would bring throngs of people from the big cities like New York. Charles and his brother, Franklin, both wanted to participate in this growth of recreation tourism. In 1853, Franklin opened a hotel in Manchester Village by combining stores, private homes and smaller hotels. He named the large luxury hotel Equinox House. It is still thriving in Manchester today.

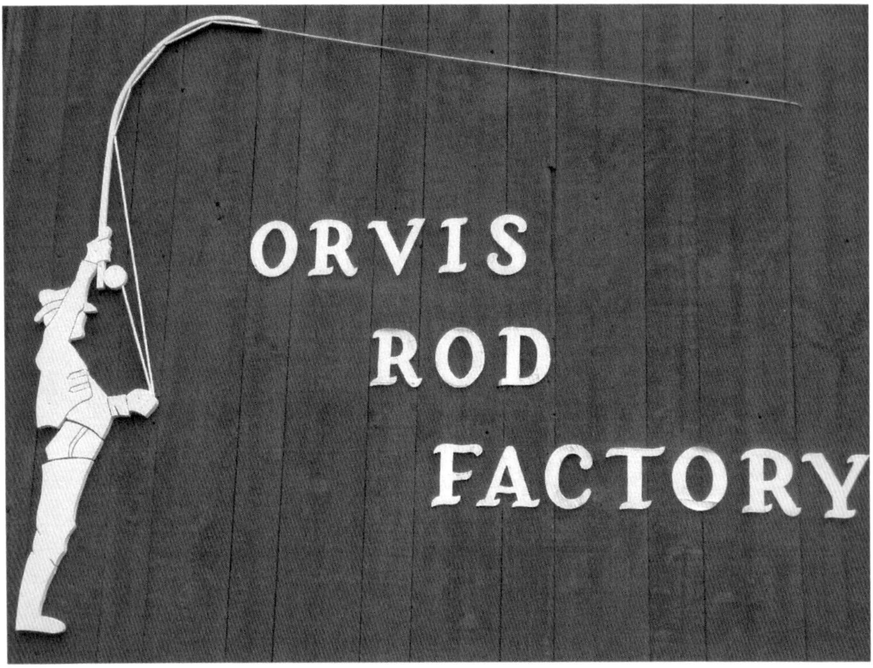

This sign is on the Orvis Fly Fishing Rod factory in Manchester. *Author's collection.*

Almost simultaneously, Charles created the Charles F. Orvis Company, turning his fishing/tackle hobby into a business. Charles Orvis was gaining a reputation as a manufacturer of quality products such as solid wood rods. To increase his business for wealthy customers, he gave them a catalogue to take home. These customers who came to fish became great advertisers. They would go home and order by mail, telling friends about Orvis fishing gear. In addition to being a retailer and outfitter, he was a mail-order merchant who made many of his own products.

It is not clear exactly when Orvis offered that first catalogue to his customers, but his shop was open in 1856 and some catalogues were apparently given out before the start of the Civil War in 1861. For comparison, some other early catalogue operations were Montgomery Ward (1872), Hammacher Schlemmer (1881) and Sears & Roebuck (1888). L.L. Bean and Eddie Bauer were started in the early 1900s.

From its beginnings in 1856, the Orvis Company grew rapidly by producing quality products and developing many first-of-a-kind products. In 1874, Orvis received a patent for the "FIRST ventilated narrow-spool fly reel to be mounted upright." In 1892, Orvis's daughter, Mary, offered a catalogue titled *Favorite Flies and Their Histories.* This catalogue was the world's FIRST illustrated classification and standardization of fishing flies. Although Charles F. Orvis died at the age of eighty-three in 1915, his legacy of innovation and firsts continued after his death.

In 1946, Orvis employees patented the FIRST impregnated bamboo rod, making the rods completely waterproof and warp proof. The rod was split in half and impregnated on the inside then glued back together. In 1966, Orvis opened the FIRST U.S. fly-fishing school in Manchester. In 1967, Orvis had both designed and produced the world's FIRST "Zinger" (pin-on-reel) for anglers. In 1972, Orvis developed the FIRST modern exposed-rim, skeleton frame, superlight fly reel and named it CFO. In 1973, he opened the FIRST dedicated wing shooting school in the United States. In the mid-1980s, the rod shop introduced the Ultra Fine, the world's FIRST two-weight graphite rod. In 1987, Orvis introduced the FIRST one-weight rod. In 1995, Orvis introduced the Trident series, the FIRST fly rod to use MVR (Maximum Vibration Reduction) technology.

The fly rod factory is still in existence in Manchester. Visitors are welcome at the fly rod factory, which is located behind the flagship retail store. Charles and Franklin Orvis are buried in Manchester Village's Dellwood Cemetery.

23

OLDEST LONG-DISTANCE HIKING TRAIL

James Paddock Taylor is generally considered the founder of Vermont's Long Trail (1910), which is now the oldest long-distance hiking trail. It predates the Appalachian Trail.

Taylor was born in Hamilton, New York, in the Finger Lakes region, on September 9, 1872. He was the son of James Morford (1843–1930) and Mary E. (Paddock) Taylor. After receiving his AB degree from Colgate University, he became a pedagogy (the art and science of teaching) instructor at Colgate in 1895–96. Taylor attended Harvard (1896–97) and Columbia (1897–98). After returning to Hamilton in 1899, he taught at the Colgate Academy until 1907. In 1908, at age thirty-six, he went to the Vermont Academy, which is located about thirty miles north of Brattleboro.

It was during his four years at the Vermont Academy that he became a champion of the cause to create a long-distance hiking trail. In his first year at Vermont Academy, Taylor had a horrible experience taking a group of students on a hike over a washed-out road to Killington Peak. Among other problems, he couldn't hike to sister mountain Pico Peak because there was no trail.

The following year, Taylor hiked to Stratton Mountain and realized there were only eight trails leading to key Vermont mountaintops. Ironically, there was none to Stratton's summit. He started to think about a trail that would connect Vermont's mountaintops, which today are well-known ski areas such as Bromley, Stratton, Killington, Pico, Stowe and Jay. He was promoting "a footpath in the wilderness" to make the Green Mountains more accessible to people.

The next year, on March 11, 1910, Taylor, along with twenty-three supporters, organized the Green Mountain Club (GMC) "to make the Vermont mountains play a larger part in the life of the people." GMC was to oversee the building and maintenance of the Long Trail.

In 1912, construction began on the Long Trail. In that year, Taylor left the Vermont Academy to work for the Greater Vermont Association as secretary in Burlington. The Greater Vermont Association became the Vermont State Chamber of Commerce in 1922. Taylor stayed in that position until his death in 1949 at age seventy-seven. Taylor's arrival in Burlington proved beneficial to Vermont. At the chamber, he promoted many environmental issues, including the beautification of Vermont roadsides.

Even though the Long Trail was not totally completed, three women successfully hiked the trail from end to end in 1927. Hiking had traditionally been more for men than women, but that did not deter the three from attempting to hike about 272 miles. Catherine Robbins, Hilda Kurth and Kathleen Norris left Williamstown, Massachusetts, on July 25, 1927, and headed north to Canada via Vermont's Long Trail. They were referred to as the Three Musketeers. Catherine Robins was from Cornwall, which is a small town near Middlebury. She had graduated from Middlebury College four years earlier. The other two women were from Schenectady, New York.

The "Three Musketeers," Kathleen Norris, Catherine Robbins and Hilda Kurth, hiking the Long Trail from end to end in 1927. *Vermont Historical Society, Barre.*

They had no Gore-Tex clothing, no iPhones and no firearms. Most importantly, they were not accompanied by men. They did have axes and three compasses each. Luckily, all their determination did not weigh anything. It took the Three Musketeers about thirty days to get to Canada. They became the FIRST women without a male escort to hike the Long Trail end to end.

It was not until 1930 that the final link was completed for the approximately 272 miles of the Long Trail from Massachusetts to Canada. With about ten thousand members, the GMC is recognized by the Vermont legislature as the "founder, sponsor, defender and protector" of the Long Trail system. The Long Trail is truly a system, with many miles of alternate side trails and spurs.

The idea for the 2,200-mile Appalachian Trail (AT) was conceived in 1921, when construction was already in progress for the Long Trail. The Long Trail and the Appalachian Trail are essentially the same now from the Massachusetts border to Route 4 by Killington. From here, the Long Trail goes north to Canada and the AT goes northeast to Maine. The GMC also maintains the AT in Vermont.

In 2014, James P. Taylor was inducted into the Vermont Sports Hall of Fame as a Historic Award Inductee.

24

FIRST NON-ENGLISHMAN TO WIN GOLFING'S BRITISH AMATEUR CHAMPIONSHIP

For a lifetime of service to golf, Walter J. Travis was a Legacy Inductee into the World Golf Hall of Fame in 1979. Travis was the FIRST three-time U.S. amateur champion and the first non-British and American person to win the British Amateur Championship.

Born in Australia on January 10, 1862, Travis moved to New York in 1986 as a twenty-four-year-old representative for an Australian company. Four years later, in 1890, he married Anne Bent of Middletown, Connecticut, and in that same year became a naturalized citizen at age twenty-eight.

In 1896, while touring England, he learned that his friends at the Niantic Club in Flushing, New York, were forming a golf club. After hearing of this new club, he bought a set of golf clubs. He stated that at age thirty-four "I first knelt at the Shrine of the Goddess of Golf." Because of his late entry into the world of golf, he was often referred to as the "Old Man" or the "Grand Old Man."

As a player, he became a dedicated, totally consumed student and self-made experimenter in the game. He finally won the U.S. Amateur Championship at age thirty-eight in 1900. He won two more times in 1901 and 1903, becoming the first to win three U.S. Amateur Championships. He was acclaimed as America's top amateur golfer, which was pretty impressive for a diminutive five-foot, seven-inch 140-pound older player. In 1904, he became the first non-British person to win the British Amateur Championship, also becoming the FIRST American to win.

In 1904, he became the FIRST man to hold the U.S. and British Amateur Championships at the same time.

Walter J. Travis is shown putting while smoking his traditional cigar. *Walter J. Travis Society.*

AS AN INNOVATIVE CONTRIBUTOR TO THE GAME

Travis was constantly trying new things. Apparently, he was the first at his home course in Garden City, New York, to install smaller, maybe half-size, cups on the putting green to improve his putting.

Travis experimented with other types of balls and designs, but in the 1901 U.S. Amateur, he used the Haskell ball with a rubber core rather than the traditional ball. That ball, which is used today with many improvements, led to lengthened golf courses.

He also experimented with shafts of different lengths, including a fifty-inch shaft to get more distance from the tee. He won the British Amateur with a "Schenectady" putter, which was new and controversial. Later, in 1910, the Royal and Ancient Golf Club at St. Andrews banned all putters it described as "mallet-head" putters (essentially those with large head surfaces), including the Schenectady. However, it would later lift that ban, as that type of putter became popular in the United States.

He shared his efforts to improve the game by writing *Practical Golf* in 1901 and *Art of Putting* in 1904. In 1908, he founded and published the *American Golfer*, the MOST authoritative golf magazine of the era.

Travis's innovative course designs were other contributions he made. He was the FIRST to really promote bunkers that were irregularly placed on the fairway rather than simply straight across. With partners, he contributed to the design of more than fifty golf courses. Some of these courses are used today for major tournaments at clubs such as Pinehurst, Pine Valley and Westchester.

In 1899, his first designed course was created for the Ekwanok Country Club in Manchester. Robert Todd Lincoln, Abraham Lincoln's only son to live to maturity, became president of the club. Travis, for his contributions to golf, was given a lifetime honorary membership in the Ekwanok Club.

Walter J. Travis died on July 31, 1927, and, by his own request, is buried in Dellwood Cemetery about three hundred yards from the Ekwanok. (His headstone is about five headstones to the right after entering the south entrance to Dellwood.)

25

FIRST AMERICAN ALPINE SKIER TO WIN TWO GOLD MEDALS IN SAME OLYMPICS

Time magazine honored Andrea Mead Lawrence for her performance at the 1952 Winter Olympics in Oslo, Norway, by featuring her on its January 21, 1952 cover. In December 1999, *Sports Illustrated* ranked her first out of the fifty greatest sports figures from Vermont.

A Vermont native, she was born in Rutland County on April 19, 1932, two months after the first Winter Olympic Games, which were held in Lake Placid, New York. She grew up in Rutland and skied at Pico ski area in Mendon, which is about fifteen minutes from Rutland. Her parents had purchased Pico. At age eleven, she joined the U.S. Alpine Ski team. At age fifteen, she competed in the 1948 Winter Olympic Games at St. Moritz, Switzerland.

At the 1952 Winter Olympic Games, she accomplished the amazing feat of winning gold medals in both the slalom and giant slalom. She was the first American alpine skier, male or female, to win two gold medals in the same Olympic Games. She was elected, at age nineteen, to be captain of the U.S. Women's Team. She also won those two events in the World Championships in that year.

Other accolades kept coming after the Oslo Winter Games. She was elected to the National Ski Hall of Fame in 1958. At the 1960 Olympic Games, she was asked to carry the torch and pass it to Olympic speed skater Ken Henry, who lit the Olympic flame. Sports facilities at Pico have been named for her. On January 10, 2013, President Obama signed the Mount Andrea Lawrence Designation Act of 2011, which named a 12,240-foot-high

The Rutland monument honoring alpine Olympic Gold Medal winner Andrea Mead Lawrence was dedicated in 2018. It is located on Merchants Row near Center Street. *Author's collection.*

peak on the John Muir Trail in California as "Mount Andrea Lawrence." In 2018, her daughter (she had five children) dedicated in downtown Rutland (corner of Merchants Row and Center Street) a beautiful marble monument with a carving of her skiing. She was inducted into the Vermont Sports Hall of Fame in 2012.

Andrea Mead was married on March 4, 1951, to David Lawrence, a fellow skier. Later in life, she moved out west and became active in environmental issues. Andrea Mead Lawrence passed away on March 30, 2009. Although records are meant to be broken, she will always be the first American alpine skier to win two gold medals in the same Olympic Games over sixty years ago.

OTHER WINTER OLYMPIANS

Vermont has had a great history of sending Olympians to the Winter Games. In fact, at the most recent 2018 Winter Games in Pyeongchang, South Korea, Vermont produced the MOST Olympians per capita in the United States by a wide margin. Vermont sent over 2.0 Olympians per

100,000 residents, with Alaska being a far second at a tad under 1.25 per 100,000. The next two states, Wyoming and Utah, sent about .5 per 100,000 each. Therefore, in Vermont, just over 2 of every 100,000 citizens is an Olympian, which writer Kevin Skiver for CBS Sports says is insane.

Three of Vermont's notable skiing firsts are presented here.

Billy Kidd was second behind Andrea Mead Lawrence on *Sports Illustrated*'s list of the fifty greatest athletes from Vermont in the twentieth century. From Stowe, he was the FIRST U.S. American man to win an Olympic Gold skiing medal, which he earned in 1964 at Innsbruck, Austria.

Bill Koch was third on *Sports Illustrated*'s list of greatest Vermont athletes. From Guilford, which is near Brattleboro, Koch was the FIRST American to win an Olympic medal in cross-country (Nordic) skiing. He accomplished this feat at the 1976 Winter Olympics, which was also held in Innsbruck, Austria.

Jessica Diggins, forty-two years after Bill Koch won the first American Nordic Olympic medal, became the FIRST American to win a Nordic Gold Medal, which she earned at the 2018 Winter Olympic Games in Pyeongchang, South Korea. She won the women's team sprint with Kikkan Randall. Jessie is a Vermont resident and trained at Stratton.

26

FIRST COMMERCIAL SKI ROPE TOW

As a ski instructor in 1933, Wallace "Bunny" Bertram was living at the famous White Cupboard Inn located in Woodstock, Windsor County, Vermont. The inn was owned by Robert and Elizabeth Royce. Business at the inn was dependent on amateur skiers, primarily from New York, coming to ski on the surrounding hills. Without any lifts, skiers would be hiking or "shinning" up the hills. People were looking for ways to encourage more skiers to visit.

Both the Royces and Bertram thought about some kind of mechanical way to get people up the mountain. They looked at options, including a mechanical lift in Canada. The next step was to map the hills around Woodstock. They worked with a topographer who identified six hills in the area and numbered them 1–6. Hill number no. 2 was chosen; at the time, it was owned by Clint Gilbert. Not surprisingly, he was a Vermont dairy farmer.

The Royces, not Bertram, paid five dollars to lease the hill for the 1934 ski season. Bertram, however, became very much involved in building that first ski rope tow lift on Gilbert's Hill. A clever arrangement was developed that ran a nine-hundred-foot-long rope tow over a wheel powered by a Model T engine. With the grandiose name White Cupboard Skyway, the lift opened on January 18, 1934, and charged one dollar per day or fifty cents for a half day. This was the first commercial rope tow in the United States. The rope tow is a predecessor to other ski tows like the Poma lift, the J bar and the T bar. The FIRST successful rider up the Woodstock rope tow is reported to have been Vermonter Bob Bourbon.

This 1934 image is of the first ski rope tow. It was located on Gilbert's Hill in Woodstock. *Woodstock History Center.*

Friction began to develop between the principal characters. When the Royces went to pay Gilbert for the next year, Bertram had already worked out a deal that included a percentage of the ticket revenues. Later, Gilbert started to think he wasn't getting an accurate count on his percentage, so Bertram severed his relationship with Gilbert. Bertram looked for another hill to ski and chose nearby hill no. 6. Making various improvements to the rope tow and purchasing more land (some very steep), Bertram was on his way to influencing U.S. skiing. The name for that hill eventually evolved into the Suicide Six Ski Area in 1937. Bertram would be associated with Suicide Six for over twenty-five years as a jack-of-all-ski-trades. Suicide Six, according to many accounts, was the BIRTHPLACE of alpine ski racing in the United States. In 1937, the Fisk Trophy Race began, and it is now the LONGEST-RUNNING alpine ski race in the United States. The FIRST youth program in the United States started at Suicide Six. Branching a little away from skiing, the FIRST snowboarding championship was held at Suicide Six.

27

OLDEST CONTINUOUSLY OPERATED GOLF COURSE

This claim is posted on a 1999 Vermont State Historic Marker near the course. The State Division of Historic Preservation does a good job of verifying the claims on its markers through a thorough independent review. The claim is also confirmed by other sources. The wording is precise on the marker, which makes no distinction between a nine-hole or an eighteen-hole course. The marker also refers to the course, not the club or the clubhouse, and does not refer to a date of incorporation or a date when a clubhouse was built.

In 1886, a group of golfers who summered in Dorset, which is next to Manchester, laid out a nine-hole golf course called the Dorset Field Links in the same location as the present club. Ten years later, in 1896, a clubhouse named Woodruff Hall was built and became the Dorset Field Club. After many alterations and improvements, including adding another nine holes in 1999, the course has been used continuously for over 130 years.

In the world of golf, there seem to be many different claims about being the oldest. *Golf Digest* indicates Dorset's claim is based on a lawyer's attest dated September 12, 1886, which was attached to a map laying out the original course. The Dorset Club's constitution and bylaws were not formalized until 1896, and incorporation wasn't formalized until 1918. When the club was "established" is open to interpretation. The *USGA Golf Journal*'s founding editor wrote in 1964 that the Dorset Field Club "may very well be the oldest golf club and course in the United States." He makes a distinction between "club" and "course."

Over twenty years later, Ross Goodner wrote in *Golf Digest*, "I think it's possible to go one step further and accept that Dorset Golf Course has been in existence since 1886 and Foxburg since 1887." The Foxburg Country Club is in Foxburg, Pennsylvania. In 1887, Foxburg built a larger course, but apparently no convincing documentation has been presented about when the first course was laid out or if it has been used continuously.

Another course, the Oakhurst Links, was designed and built in 1884 by Russell Montegue and friends. He designed his course outside his home in White Sulphur Springs, West Virginia. Clearly, it is the oldest course, and it is listed in the National Register of Historic Places. However, it has not been in continuous operation. It was open from 1884 to 1912 but then it became pasture and was not restored until over eighty years later in 1994.

Summarizing everything, the Dorset Field Club claim that it is the "oldest continually operated golf course in the United States" is a valid claim supported by documentation and golf experts.

28
FIRST LUXURY RESORT IN ADIRONDACKS

Apollos Smith was born about fifteen miles outside of Burlington in Milton on August 20, 1825. Milton is on Lake Champlain. With an adventurous Vermont spirit, at the age of sixteen, he left home and worked on a Lake Champlain canalboat. These boats were new and somewhat unique to Lake Champlain, as the Lake Champlain canal had recently opened in 1819. To work on these boats required a love of the outdoors, strength and agility. As a true Vermonter, Smith loved hunting and fishing, which he continued to enjoy in the Adirondacks when he had time away from the canalboat.

As a result, he became a well-known hunting and fishing guide in the Loon Lake region of the Adirondacks. In 1848, at age twenty-three, with help from his parents, he started a small hotel near Loon Lake. Four years later, he built a primitive "Hunter's Home" that was popular with visiting professionals from eastern cities. In 1858, with some financial help from some of these professional customers, he bought land on Lower St. Regis Lake and started building a luxury hotel with seventeen bedrooms and opulent furnishings.

The hotel expanded to 225 rooms and had a bowling alley, a casino and a stable for over fifty horses. Apollos Smith, more generally known as Paul Smith, built and managed the first large luxury hotel in the Adirondack Mountains. Within the Adirondack Mountains, Adirondack Park was formally established in 1892. The six-million-acre park was the first of its kind, encompassing both public and private land. The Apollos Smith Hotel became known as Paul Smith's Hotel, and the surrounding town was named Paul Smiths.

Apollos "Paul" Smith's hotel in the Adirondack Mountains, circa 1903. *Library of Congress, Prints and Photograph Division.*

In the early 1900s, Paul Smith was starting to sell off some of his vast holdings to his wealthy clients. One such client and friend was Archibald White, who purchased thirty-five lakefront acres in 1907. He built a "camp" with twenty original buildings, a bowling alley and many other amenities. The White Pine Camp was a short boat ride or less than three miles from Paul Smith's Hotel. Paul Smith died in 1912. In 1920, White Pine was sold to Laura and Irwin Kirkwood. Laura was a friend of First Lady Grace Coolidge. When Laura died, Irwin offered the camp to the president and Mrs. Coolidge. For two and a half months, White Pine was the summer White House for Calvin Coolidge.

The hotel burned down in 1930. Paul's son, Phelps, left the entire estate to establish a college on the site of the hotel. Paul Smith's College started accepting students in 1946. Both White Pine and Paul Smith's College are thriving today.

29

FIRST DOCUMENTED INTERNATIONAL ICE HOCKEY GAME

On February 26, 1886, during the Burlington Carnival of Winter Sports, an ice hockey game was played between the Montreal Hockey Club (the Crystals) and a local Burlington-area team. Montreal won 3–0. The game was played on the Lake Champlain waterfront on a Central Vermont Railroad Wharf. It is not clear when the transition to round pucks happened, but a square puck was used at least until 1885. This first documented ice hockey game may have used a square puck.

On October 5, 2019, a Vermont State Historic Marker was dedicated to memorialize this event in Burlington.

VII

RELIGION

30

FIRST AND ONLY CARTHUSIAN MONASTERY IN THE UNITED STATES

Famous for Chartreuse liqueur, the Carthusian Order is a Catholic order of monastics that built its first hermitage in the Chartreuse Mountains of the French Alps. The order was founded in France in 1084 by Saint Bruno. The monasteries are also referred to by the English name *charterhouses*. The alcoholic drink, which is only produced at the Grande Chartreuse in France, has also given rise to the color chartreuse.

As recently as 2018, there were fewer than twenty-five existing charterhouses throughout the world, including the mother house. Most charterhouses are in Europe.

The lone U.S. charterhouse is in Vermont in Sandgate, Bennington County. The story of how the monks built the Sandgate charterhouse starts with the monks themselves. Some religious families live in communities like the Benedictines, but others live in greater solitude like the Carthusians. Solitude is the main Carthusian theme and is viewed as a privilege of becoming intimate with God. The solitude is reflected in the physical construction and locations of the charterhouses. There are a series of cells (hermitages) that are attached by a cloister, which ends in a communal area. Although silent most of the time, monks do take weekly walks, when they are allowed to speak.

The U.S. Carthusians originally settled temporarily in southern Vermont (Windham County) in the Wilmington area. However, since they were near a road, it was noisy and did not meet the Carthusians' desire for their cherished silence. They were looking for another site to build a charterhouse.

The Carthusian monks' Charterhouse of the Transfiguration in Sandgate, Vermont. *Author's collection.*

This brings us to Dr. Joseph George Davidson, who was born on February 7, 1892, in New York City. Dr. Davidson was an esteemed businessman and scientist who had a doctorate in chemistry from Columbia University. As president of the Chemical Division of Union Carbide, he had also been working on the atom bomb in Oak Ridge, Tennessee. Davidson retired in 1960 and continued to be active in Vermont as a director of the National Life Insurance Company, a trustee of the University of Vermont and chairman of Putnam Memorial Hospital in Bennington.

Prior to retirement, Davidson started to buy vacant land in 1939 on Equinox Mountain, the tallest mountain in the Taconic range near Arlington, Vermont. He eventually bought enough land to essentially own Equinox Mountain. Just before World War II, he began building a private road to the top of Mount Equinox. That road, which was not completed until 1947, is over five miles long and the LONGEST solely private paved road in the United States. Davidson also proposed a ski area for Mount Equinox, but because of nearby Bromley Ski Area opening and extreme weather on Mount Equinox, he dropped the plan. He also wanted to build a funicular to the top from what is now the Southern Vermont Arts Center in Manchester, but that idea was also abandoned.

In the 1950s, before his full retirement, Dr. Davidson met Brother Paul Diamond of the Carthusians in Wilmington, who was inquiring about a possible hydroelectric plant on Mount Equinox. Dr. Davidson and his wife, Madeline, became friends with Brother Diamond over the ensuing years. The Davidsons had no children and were fond of the Carthusians, so they began transferring and bequeathing small land parcels to the Carthusians on Mount Equinox. Eventually, around seven thousand acres had been transferred, and the Carthusians had begun building their modern charterhouse on the west side of Mount Equinox in a quiet, forested mountain valley area. The Charterhouse of the Transfiguration was built with granite from Barre. The official house opening in 1970 permitted the public to visit the monastery, for the first and last time.

Unfortunately, Joseph George Davidson was unable to attend the 1970 grand opening. He died on October 9, 1969, at Putnam Memorial Hospital in Bennington. Putnam Memorial Hospital evolved into the Southwestern Medical Center. Today home to fewer than twenty monks, the Charterhouse of the Transfiguration is the only Carthusian charterhouse in the United States and remains closed to the public. However, the public can see the charterhouse from the toll road to the top of Mount Equinox, which is accessible off Route 7A in Sunderland.

31

FIRST TWO PRESIDENTS OF THE MORMON CHURCH

Joseph Smith Jr.

Joseph Smith Jr. was born on December 23, 1805, in Sharon, about ten miles from Norwich in Windsor County. Joseph Smith Jr.'s father, Joseph Smith Sr., and mother, Lucy, both had religious backgrounds. Lucy was a Congregationalist, and her father, Ansel, believed in Universalism. Joseph Smith Sr.'s father, Asael, was associated with Rationalism and Seekerism, which seemed to reject organized religion altogether. Joseph Smith Sr. thought some dreams were divine messages communicated by God.

People in New England from the early 1800s to the 1840s were becoming religious conscious, and Vermont was part of that interest. This was the period of the Second Great Awakening. Traveling ministers, as in the First Great Awakening, were going to small towns and having camp meetings.

In 1812, when Joseph Smith Jr. was only seven, he was diagnosed with life-threatening typhoid. Although there was talk of leg amputation, Smith was saved by the removal of some of his bones. However, he became crippled and had to use crutches for three years.

Joseph Smith Sr. had been a successful farmer, but after some bad business ventures, the family ended up essentially as poor tenant farmers. After several crop failures, Joseph Smith Sr. moved the family to Western New York (Palmyra). Joseph Smith Jr. was around eleven or twelve years old. By this time, he had become interested in religion. Palmyra was an area of great religious fervor during the Second Great Awakening. When he was still a teenager, Joseph Smith Jr. is said to have experienced several visions. One vision when he was fifteen years old was of God the Father and Jesus Christ. Another vision when he was eighteen years old was of an angel who directed him to locate a buried book of golden plates.

Joseph Smith Jr., first president of the Church of Latter-day Saints. *Library of Congress.*

After publishing the Book of Mormon, which Smith claimed was the English translation of those plates, the Mormon religion was formally founded in 1830. Joseph Smith Jr., at age twenty-four, was the first president of the church. In 1831, Smith and his followers moved west to Ohio, Missouri and Illinois, but after many years of persecution, he was caught up in an anti-Mormon fervor. While in an Illinois jail, he was shot and killed by a mob on June 27, 1844. He was only thirty-nine years old.

Although Joseph Smith Jr. was only about twelve years old when he left Vermont, he asserted that his Vermont childhood, according to author Vance Savage, had essentially shaped his character: "It is a love of liberty which inspired my soul—civil and religious liberty to the whole human race."

In Sharon, Joseph Smith Jr.'s birthplace is a National Historic Site. The obelisk that marks the spot of his birth is made of Vermont granite.

BRIGHAM YOUNG

Brigham Young was born on June 1, 1801, in Whittingham, which is in southern Vermont's Windham County. He was about four years older than Joseph Smith Jr. Like Joseph Smith Jr., he too had been caught up in religious fervor of the Second Great Awakening in New England. Brigham needed employment to survive, so he became a traveling carpenter and blacksmith.

By age twenty-eight, Brigham Young had moved to Mendon, New York, and his interest in religion continued. Mendon is about twenty miles from Palmyra, where the Smith family had moved. The Book of Mormon was published in 1830, and it was so inspiring to Young that, two years later, on April 14, 1832, Young was baptized into the Mormon Church. Later, in 1838, the church was renamed the Church of Jesus Christ of Latter-day Saints.

The Brigham Young memorial in Whittingham, Vermont. *Author's collection.*

In 1844, Young heard that Joseph Smith Jr. had been killed in Illinois, so he returned to Illinois. At the time, there was a period of uncertainty in church organizations with spinoff denominations. Some thought there should be a "protector" as opposed to a president. However, Young was ordained as the second president of the church in December 1847. Brigham Young then led the Mormons to Utah. He would remain president until his death in 1877. During his period in Utah, Young also became governor of the territory.

32

FIRST ORDAINED AFRICAN AMERICAN PASTOR

Lemuel Haynes's remarkable story starts in West Hartford, Connecticut, when he was born on July 18, 1753, to a Caucasian mother and black father. It is not clear what the exact family situation was, but at age five months, Lemuel ended up in Granville, Massachusetts, as an indentured servant to a blind farmer, Deacon David Rose, and his wife. Part of the terms of Rose's obligation was to educate Lemuel and bring him to church. While with the Roses, Haynes became familiar with Calvinistic teachings. In 1774, Lemuel's indenture period expired. He joined the minutemen of Granville, Massachusetts, which is located north of Hartford.

In 1776, Haynes marched to Fort Ticonderoga to help garrison the fort that Ethan Allen and the Green Mountain Boys had captured the prior year. He was one of three African Americans assigned to Ethan Allen's Green Mountain Boys. During the American Revolution, he started writing about slavery and its relationship to life, liberty and the pursuit of happiness.

After his military service, Haynes studied theology in Connecticut and Massachusetts; he received his license to preach in 1780. He preached in the Congregational church in Granville, becoming the FIRST African American to minister to an all-white congregation.

It was around 1780 that he served as a missionary in the wilderness of Vermont. Three years before, on July 8, 1777, Vermont had ratified its constitution to become an independent republic. That constitution banned slavery in Vermont. People poured into the independent-thinking Vermont, which had become the "northern frontier."

Vermont Division of Historic Preservation historic marker in West Rutland honoring Lemuel Haynes. It is near where his church was located. *Author's collection.*

Finally, in 1785, Haynes was ordained and became the pastor of the Hemlock Congregational Church in Torrington, Connecticut, on the Connecticut River. He became the first African American to be ordained in the United States. In 1787, he was called to be pastor of West Parish Church in Rutland, Vermont. In 1804, Middlebury College bestowed on him an honorary master of arts degree, which was the FIRST for an African American.

In 1818, after thirty years in West Rutland, he resigned and took a temporary position in Manchester, Vermont. After about three years in Manchester, he moved to South Granville, New York, near the Vermont border, to be pastor at the South Granville Congregational Church. He served there from 1822 until he died in 1833 at the age of eighty. He is buried in the Lee-Oatman Cemetery in South Granville. He married a white schoolteacher and had over ten children. His home is a National Historic Landmark in South Granville, New York.

Mark Bushnell's book *Hidden History of Vermont* (The History Press, 2017) presents a very interesting and concise chapter on Lemuel Haynes.

VIII

LAW

33

FIRST WRONGFUL MURDER CONVICTION

In 1812, two brothers, Jesse and Stephen Boorn, were seen fighting in a field on the Boorn farm in Manchester with their brother-in-law Russell Colvin. Having accused Colvin of being a slacker, the Boorn brothers evidently never got along with him. Russell Colvin was also not the brightest person in town, and that fight in the field was the last time anyone saw him alive. (Sometimes Boorn is spelled Bourne.)

After seven years of little action in the case, Amos Boorn, the uncle of the suspects, had a dream and claimed Russell Colvin had appeared next to his bed saying that his remains had been put in a cellar hole in a potato field on the Boorn farm. The hole was excavated, and sure enough, they found a penknife, a jackknife and other items. No remains were found. Russell Colvin's wife, Sally Boorn Colvin, identified these items as her husband's possessions. However, she had a real incentive to have him declared dead because she had given birth to a baby that was not Russell's child.

Subsequently, a dog dug up bone fragments that three local physicians pronounced as human, but not necessarily Russell Colvin's remains. Later, there were rumors of the Boorn brothers burying Colvin then digging him up and reburying him. Everything was speculation with no factual basis.

Seven years after the fight in the field, witnesses claimed hearing the Boorn brothers threaten to kill Colvin. Therefore, seven years after the fight, Jesse Boorn was arrested, and a warrant was put out for Stephen Boorn, who had moved to New York. The farce continued. While in jail, a cellmate, Silas Merrill, who was an alleged forger, claimed that Jesse had

A middle section of Manchester's Equinox Hotel. This section was originally Captain Black's Tavern, which also housed court offices in the early 1800s. *Author's collection.*

blamed his brother Stephen for clubbing Colvin during the argument and Jesse then cut Colvin's throat with a penknife. Of course, Silas said he would testify against the brothers in exchange for his immediate release. Merrill, in fact, was set free.

The story gets even better. Hoping to save himself, Jesse confessed but put most of the blame on his brother Stephen, whom he thought was safely outside of Vermont in New York. However, a constable got Stephen back to Vermont, and Jesse recanted his confession. The trial went forward with the death penalty for both. Desperate for a plea bargain, Stephen confessed but said it was only in self-defense. Another twist occurred when the physicians changed their story and said the bones were not human as they had said seven years before.

For the trial, the Boorn brothers' defense attorneys were Richard Skinner and Leonard Sargent. Skinner would go on to be governor of Vermont the following year, 1820. Leonard Sargent would go on to be a Vermont representative and senator in the 1830s. (Both men are buried in Dellwood Cemetery in Manchester.)

Like everyone else, even the defense lawyers assumed the Boorn brothers might be guilty. At the trial, the chief justice was Dudley Chase, former U.S.

senator from Vermont. In the end, it was the witnesses, not any associated evidence such as a body, who convicted both Boorn brothers and sentenced them to death. Jesse was given life imprisonment, but not Stephen.

It gets weirder. A November 26, 1819 newspaper article about the murder in the famous *New York Evening Post* was read aloud in the lobby of a New York hotel. A visitor, Tabor Chadwick from New Jersey, heard it and said he knew a man named Russell Colvin who lived in New Jersey. This man met the description of the Vermonter Russell Colvin. Chadwick wrote a letter to the *Post* that was published on December 6, 1819.

A Manchester native living in New York who had read the letter to the *Post* went to New Jersey and, using deception, got Colvin to return to Manchester. People were stunned to see Russell Colvin alive. However, after seven years, many people who knew him had left town, so an identification hearing (court of inquiry) was held in the court offices on the second floor of Captain Black's Tavern (now part of the Equinox Hotel). It was concluded that the dead Russell Colvin was in fact alive. The Boorn brothers were finally set free and exonerated.

The Gerald McFarland book *The Counterfeit Man* (Notable Trials Library, 2000) makes fascinating reading on this case and gives inside information on why this wrongful death conviction could take place in the early 1800s in Vermont. Many of the sites mentioned in the book are still in existence.

34

ONLY STATE WITH LAY "SIDE JUDGES"

The concept of an extralegal "side judge" who sits on the side of the presiding judge in a Vermont trial goes back to the very foundation of Vermont.

When Vermont declared its independence on July 8, 1777, it had to form its own legal framework. Because there were very few resident Vermont judges, the young republic had to rely on traveling or circuit judges to handle cases both civil and criminal. Many of these judges were from New York. It was a Vermonter, Ethan Allen, who had captured Fort Ticonderoga in New York, where Vermonters were not well liked. Additionally, many lawyers supported New York in the ongoing land disputes. In summary, there was little trust of outside judges. Also, if a judge was from outside Vermont, Vermonters didn't feel the judge would know local standards or customs.

Therefore, to address these concerns, the 1777 Vermont Constitution allowed for two assistant judges who were lay side judges to ensure that pro-British or pro–New York judges could not control the independent Vermont court system. To guarantee local input, the side judges were elected by the people of Vermont with two per county.

These lay side judges had input into issues like "matters of fact." They were familiar with local customs and the physical area itself. They also knew the people. These local judges provided outsider traveling judges with additional facts and considerations, while assuring local residents that they were represented by local people for the trial.

The 1822 courthouse in Manchester with its two side judge chairs is a good example of a centuries-old tradition. *Author's collection.*

Gradually, in Vermont, side judges' power has been reduced, and now they can no longer rule in criminal cases or any trial by jury. There have been pressures over time to eliminate side judges, but there are still many people who think this type of judge has a role in the courthouse. Dick Sears, Bennington County senator, stated, "Assistant Judges are important because they are a link to the public....They know the communities, and in an age where you have judges who rotate, there isn't that same familiarity....I think they perform an important judiciary function. They take some of the work load off of the sitting judge. They also become better trained over the years. I've seen improvements."

Acting as assistant judges, side judges also prepare budgets, deal with the county sheriff's office and perform other management functions. Courts are allowed to proceed with only one or no assistant judges, but their input is restricted to matters of fact, not law. When appropriate, the vote of a side judge is the same as the presiding judge.

35

FIRST SHARED CUSTOMS BUILDING

The U.S.-Canadian International Boundary is about 5,500 miles long, including the Alaska-Canada border, making it the longest international border in the world between two countries. Disputes between the countries have been settled peacefully. There have been many treaties to settle disputes concerning the exact border, but many of those disputes were essentially settled in 1783 with the Treaty of Paris. This treaty settled the border at the 45th parallel of north longitude. However, the Vermont-Canada border is actually entirely above the 45th parallel and, in some cases, over a mile above the 45th parallel. The Alburgh-Noyan crossing is actually at 45.01151° longitude.

Continuing on the theme of peace and cooperation, in 1992, a single building for both U.S. and Canadian inspection stations was built. Previously, in 1900, the crossing on Route VT225 had separate facilities. The U.S. building had been erected in 1934. The 1992 building was the first shared facility on the U.S.-Canada border. It is on the ninety-mile border that Vermont shares with Canada. The U.S. Customs and Border Protection (CBP) Agency manages the interests of the United States. The CBP has over sixty thousand employees, making it one of the world's largest law enforcement organizations. Border protection also includes agriculture inspection to ensure no pests or disease are allowed to enter the United States.

There was considerable logic to having a shared building at this crossing. This crossing was important but lightly traveled, with twenty cars a day

This shared U.S.-Canada customshouse is at the Alburg-Noyan border crossing. *Author's collection.*

or fewer. The agencies on both sides did not want to maintain full-time buildings year-round because maintenance during Vermont and Canadian winters can be expensive. Therefore, sharing seemed logical.

The physical geographic crossing is also unique, as it is on the Alburgh "Tongue," which juts down from Canada into Lake Champlain. This meant Alburgh itself is surrounded by water, and it's necessary to cross parts of Lake Champlain to get to the crossing. This geographical feature meant it might be easier to control if there were any issues. As a side, some other Vermont "crossings" are unique. The line in the famous Haskell Library in Derby Line cuts the library reading room in half.

This first shared crossing has been successful, and as a result, over five more have been built based on the Vermont Alburg-Noyan model. The name Alburgh was spelled with a final -h, but in 1891, the federal government suggested, for simplicity, that towns with the -burgh should drop the *H*. However, on town meeting day in 2006, the town voted to go back to the Alburgh spelling. The federal crossing kept the shorter version, Alburg.

36

SOLE AUTHOR OF THE U.S. THIRTEENTH AMENDMENT

The Academy Award–winning Best Picture film *Lincoln* starring Daniel Day-Lewis and Sally Field was based almost entirely on how President Abraham Lincoln engineered the passing of the Thirteenth Amendment, which banned slavery.

The sole author of that amendment was Jacob Merritt Howard, who was born on July 10, 1805, in Shaftsbury, which is in southern Vermont's Bennington County. Howard's parents were Otis Howard and Mary "Polly" Millington. His father was a farmer. Howard's education included schools in Shaftsbury, Brattleboro and Bennington—all in southern Vermont. Vermont had only been a state for about thirty years, and schools were proud of Vermont being the first state to ban slavery.

For college, Howard attended Williams in Williamstown, Massachusetts, which is just over the border from Vermont. In 1830, at age twenty-five, he graduated as a member of Phi Beta Kappa, studied law and then moved to Detroit in 1832 when he was twenty-seven years old.

Howard went on to be elected to the Michigan House of Representatives. Almost always an antislavery abolitionist, he became increasingly uncomfortable with his Whig Party. In 1854, he wrote the resolutions that were adopted on July 6 at a convention that founded the Republican Party. He was elected a U.S. senator from Michigan as a Republican in 1862 and served until his death in 1871.

Howard was serving in the U.S. Senate during the Civil War years. Lincoln realized that he had a problem. His Emancipation Proclamation, effective

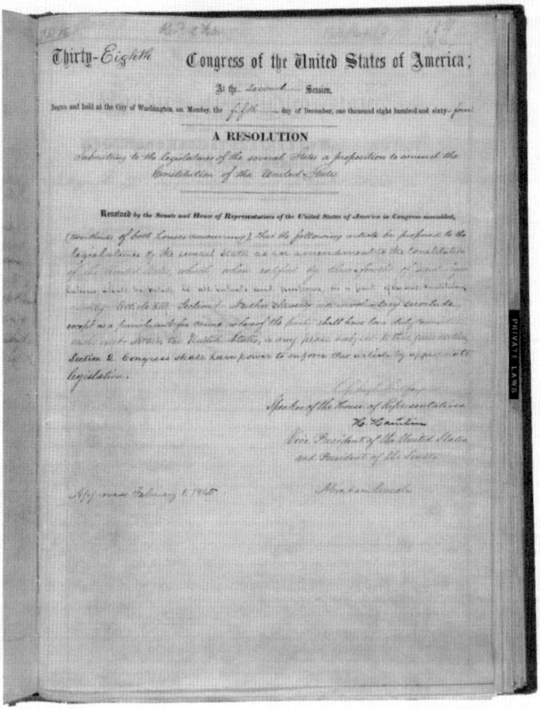

Thirty-Eighth Congress of the United States of America;

At the Second Session.

Begun and held at the City of Washington, on Monday, the fifth day of December, one thousand eight hundred and sixty-four.

A RESOLUTION

Resolved by the Senate and House of Representatives of the United States of America in Congress assembled,

The original Thirteenth Amendment banning slavery that passed the U.S. House with Abraham Lincoln's signature at the bottom. *Library of Congress.*

January 1, 1863, was a wartime act and might not carry over in peacetime. Some of the states in the Union had legal slavery. Lincoln recognized that the ban on slavery must be permanent and a part of the Constitution that would apply to all states.

The task of choosing the correct words for a Thirteenth Amendment that would abolish slavery and get approved and passed by three-fourths of the states was no easy task. As background, in February 1861, Congress did pass a Thirteenth Amendment, but it was to perpetuate slavery, not to end it. However, the Civil War broke out, and the states could not ratify that amendment.

Working with Lincoln, Howard crafted forty-four words that they thought could pass in Congress.

> *Article 1: Neither slavery nor involuntary servitude, except as a punishment for crime whereof the party shall have been duly convicted, shall exist within the United States, or any place subject to their jurisdiction.*
> *Article 2: Congress shall have the power to enforce this article with appropriate legislation.*

In 1864, a year before the Civil War ended, the U.S. Senate passed the amendment 38–6, but in the House of Representatives, it was defeated 93–65. Abolishing slavery was almost solely a Republican cause. Only four Democrats voted for the amendment. Passing the Thirteenth Amendment became part of Lincoln's Republican platform for the upcoming election.

The amendment wording and Lincoln's efforts worked. In January 1865, with a vote of 119–56, the amendment passed in the House. Lincoln also insisted that all states, before they return to the Union, ratify the amendment. Vermont, on March 9, 1865, voted 207–0 to ratify the Thirteenth Amendment. Unfortunately, Lincoln was assassinated in April 1865 before the amendment was ratified on December 6, 1865.

Jacob Merritt Howard died on April 2, 1871, at age sixty-five. There is a Vermont Division of Historic Preservation marker in Shaftsbury memorializing Jacob Merritt Howard as being the sole author of the Thirteenth Amendment.

37

FIRST STATE TO LEGISLATE SAME-SEX CIVIL UNIONS

In the late 1990s, Vermont was trying to develop a methodology for same-sex couples to obtain the same legal rights and responsibilities as a married couple would have. The wording of proposed legislation was finalized, and the legislature approved it. In July 2000, Vermont became the first state to allow civil unions between people of the same sex. In the following year, almost 2,500 same-sex couples took advantage of Vermont's civil union legislation. Only 20 percent were Vermont residents.

Although Vermont was not the first to legalize same-sex marriages, in 2009, it was the FIRST to do so without a court order.

38

FIRST STATE TO LEGISLATE ABSENTEE VOTING

Vermont, on November 24, 1896, became the first state to allow for absentee voting. The law did not allow some of the broad absentee voting options of today. However, it did allow a voter in the state to vote at any polling place other than the voter's normal polling place.

Earlier, during the Civil War (1861–1865), some soldiers were allowed to vote if they were away. However, this voting was not enacted through state legislation.

39

FIRST TO PROHIBIT SIT-DOWN STRIKES

During the Great Depression, Vermont's main quarry towns were Proctor and Barre. In Barre, there was great agitation from granite workers for increased wages during the early 1930s. Many were unionized, and there was even a two-month strike in 1933.

At Proctor's Vermont Marble Company, more than one hundred quarrymen struck on October 18, 1935, when management wanted to cut their wages by reducing hours. The situation became ugly. At least one thousand workers marched through Proctor in December. There were clashes between opposing sides, resulting in injuries as the strike wore on for over four months.

The Vermont legislature finally got involved and sided with management. On April 7, 1937, Vermont passed legislation that banned sit-down strikes, when workers stop working but remain in the facility until a settlement is reached. This was the first law banning sit-down strikes in the United States. Later, George Aiken, not happy with the bill he signed as governor, would create a Department of Labor at the state level to help settle later strikes. Maybe he had a little signer's remorse.

IX

CALVIN COOLIDGE

40

FIRSTS FOR THE CALVIN COOLIDGE FAMILY

There are so many firsts for the Calvin Coolidge family that the Coolidges deserve a separate chapter. To start, by being born on July 4, 1872, in Plymouth Notch, Calvin Coolidge was the FIRST U.S. president and, as of this writing, the ONLY president born on Independence Day.

Coolidge's childhood home was in Plymouth Notch across the street from where he was born. He attended the Black River Academy in Ludow but then left Vermont to attend Amherst College in Massachusetts. After college, starting with local offices, he worked his way up in government to become governor of Massachusetts from January 2, 1919, to January 6, 1921. While governor, he was chosen to be the vice-presidential running mate of presidential candidate Warren Harding. Harding won the election, and from March 4, 1921, to August 2, 1923, Coolidge served as vice president of the United States. During this period as VP, he was the first VP to sit in on cabinet meetings. The office of VP had previously been considered more of a ceremonial position.

On August 2, 1923, President Harding died suddenly while Vice President Coolidge was vacationing at his family home in Plymouth Notch. At 2:40 a.m. on August 3, Colonel John Coolidge, a justice of the peace and notary public, swore Calvin Coolidge in as president. The ceremony was held in President Coolidge's childhood home, as his father managed the family farm. This was the FIRST time a U.S. president was sworn in by his father.

While president from August 3, 1923, to March 4, 1929, Coolidge had several other notable and interesting firsts. Coolidge chose not to run for

John Coolidge swearing in his son Calvin on August 3, 1923, early in the morning in Plymouth Notch. That room is in the childhood home of President Calvin Coolidge. Grace Coolidge was one of the witnesses. *Library of Congress.*

reelection in 1928 for a second elected term. Shortly after he was sworn in, he made the FIRST presidential speech on national radio by allowing his address to Congress to be broadcast nationally. In 1924, on August 24, Coolidge became the FIRST president to be in a sound movie when he spoke in a four-minute film titled *Calvin Coolidge; Taken on the White House Grounds*.

In 1928, Coolidge named the FIRST woman, Genevieve R. Cline, to the federal judiciary by assigning her to the U.S. Customs Court. Inconsistent with his "Silent Cal" image, over the course of his presidency, he held over five hundred press conferences. Until 2006, this was the most press conferences by any president. However, over recent years, the definition of a "press conference" has evolved. For instance, presidents now give informal press conferences on Air Force One flights.

Grace Anna Goodhue, the vivacious wife of Silent Cal, contributed her own firsts to the Coolidge legacy. Born in Burlington, she was the FIRST and, as of this writing, the ONLY first lady born in Vermont. Grace graduated from the University of Vermont (UVM). While at UVM, she was a founding member of Pi Beta Phi, the FIRST national fraternity for women. As first lady,

First Lady Grace Coolidge with her pet raccoon Rebecca. *Library of Congress, Prints and Photographs Division, Harris and Ewing Collection.*

Grace would have the FIRST and ONLY raccoons as presidential pets. The first raccoon was named Rebecca. Rebecca had been sent from Mississippi to be part of the White House Thanksgiving dinner in 1926, but the Coolidges kept her as a pet. Later, they were given another raccoon named Reuben, thinking Rebecca needed company. Apparently, Rebecca and Reuben didn't get along. In total, between Grace and Calvin, they had the MOST pets of any presidential couple. They also had goats, dogs, canaries, a bobcat and a donkey. Under Coolidge, the White House was sometimes referred to as the Pennsylvania Avenue Zoo.

One of the best places to experience these Coolidge firsts is the Calvin Coolidge State Historic Site. The area is also a National Historic Landmark District. In Plymouth Notch, Vermont, the visitor can stand in one spot and see the house where a president was born, where he grew up, where he was sworn in and where he had his first Summer White House. That spot is the ONLY place in the world you can see all of those events in the life of a U.S. president. In addition, a short distance away is Calvin Coolidge's burial site. In its simplicity, the entire rural landmark site is impressive.

X

ARTS

41

LARGEST COLLECTION OF GRANDMA MOSES PAINTINGS

The famous painter Anna Mary Robertson Moses, who was lovingly referred to as Grandma Moses, was born in 1860 in Greenwich, New York, near Bennington. Not only does the Bennington Museum have the largest collection of Grandma Moses paintings but part of the museum is the original schoolhouse in which Grandma Moses attended school as a young girl as well. The Grandma Moses collection also includes many artifacts from her life, including her school chair and other paraphernalia. Other public collections of Grandma Moses paintings are with the Metropolitan Museum of Art (NY), Brooklyn Museum (NY) and the Smithsonian American Art Museum (Washington, D.C.).

Numerous accolades to Grandma Moses indicate what an important painter she became in portraying rural America. In 1939, three Grandma Moses paintings were included in New York's Museum of Modern Art exhibition titled *Contemporary Unknown American Painters*. In 1940, fifty of her paintings were displayed at New York's famous Gimbels department store. Over the next twenty years, her paintings were exhibited throughout Europe and the United States. In 1950, the National Press Club recognized her as one of the five most "newsworthy" women in the country. When she was eighty-eight, *Mademoiselle* magazine named her a "Young Woman of the Year." She was awarded two honorary doctoral degrees. President Truman presented her with the National Press Club award for accomplishment in art in 1949. In 2006, her 1943 work *Sugaring Off* sold at auction for over $1

The Grandma Moses Schoolhouse with its large collection of Grandma Moses paintings and artifacts is part of the Bennington Museum. *Author's collection.*

million. Grandma Moses was honored with a 1969 commemorative postage stamp including her name and her painting *Fourth of July*. Her home in Virginia was listed in the National Register of Historic Places in 2012. An autobiography, *My Life's History*, won numerous awards. Over Moses's short remarkable life as an artist, she painted over 1,500 works.

This list of accomplishments in the art world is made even more remarkable by the fact she really didn't start painting until she was in her 70s. She died in 1961 at the age of 101.

Anna Mary Robertson Moses was the third of ten children and was raised with five brothers and four sisters. Her father was a farmer who ran a flax mill. In her youth, she attended a one-room school for a short period. At age twelve, she left home to work for a wealthy neighboring farmer. She worked in the Vermont and New York area for the next fifteen years. She met a fellow farmhand, Thomas Salmond Moses, and at age twenty-seven, they married. They then went to Virginia, where they would spend another twenty years working on different farms. Only five of her ten children survived beyond infancy.

In 1905, the couple returned to Eagle Bridge, New York, a town near where she grew up. She was sixty-seven when her husband died. Later, she developed arthritis, which made embroidering difficult, prompting the turn in her mid-seventies to a painting career.

Her style features scenes of simple, old-fashioned, rural life. She omitted elements of current modern life such as TV antennas, telephone poles and tractors. She wanted future generations to know how "we" lived.

As a side note, from 1939 to 1952, Norman Rockwell lived in Arlington, Vermont, which is within twenty miles of where Grandma Moses lived. They were good friends, and both artists painted Americana scenes.

42

FIRST AND ONLY POET TO WIN FOUR PULITZER PRIZES FOR POETRY

Robert Frost was born in San Francisco on March 26, 1874. After Frost's father died in 1885, when Frost was nearly eleven years old, he moved east to Lawrence, Massachusetts. His grandfather, a manager in a mill, was looking after the family. After graduating from Lawrence High School in 1892 at eighteen years old, Frost attended Dartmouth College for two months in Hanover, New Hampshire.

In 1894, just two years after graduating from high school, he sold his first poem: "My Butterfly: An Elegy." In 1895, Frost married Elinor White in Lawrence, Massachusetts.

Frost attended Harvard from 1897 to 1899 but left early due to health issues. Frost's grandfather purchased a farm for Robert and Elinor in Derry, New Hampshire, which he worked for nine years. Farming proved unsuccessful, so he returned to the field of education as an English teacher at New Hampshire's Pinkerton Academy from 1906 to 1911 and then to Plymouth (NH) State University, which was a normal school at the time. When Frost's poem "A Boy's Will" was published, it earned him enough money to buy a farm in northern New Hampshire, Franconia, where he could dedicate himself to writing, teaching and lecturing.

When Robert Frost was about forty-six, he started living in a colonial-era house in Shaftsbury, Vermont, just north of Bennington, where he had planned on having an orchard. He would have the house throughout the 1920s. Since he now lived in Vermont, Frost spent almost every summer and fall between 1921 and 1962 at Middlebury College's mountain campus in Addison County's Ripton. Breadloaf, the name of his Ripton farmhouse,

The Robert Frost house in Shaftsbury where he composed "Stopping by the Woods on a Snowy Evening." *Author's collection.*

is now a National Historic Landmark. Throughout his life, Frost traveled and lived in many places, but he always retained a deep rural Vermont connection. Robert Frost had a Vermont connection for over forty-two years before he died in 1963 at age eighty-eight.

Frost's writings are somewhat simple, have a rural flavor and make use of considerable colloquial language. Frost's four Pulitzer Prizes for Poetry were

1923: *New Hampshire: A Poem with Notes and Grace Notes*
1931: *Collected Poems*
1937: *A Further Range*
1943: *A Witness Tree*

While in Shaftsbury during the early 1920s, Frost composed many pieces that eventually became the *New Hampshire* collection. One of those poems was the famous masterpiece "Stopping by the Woods on a Snowy Evening." It is ironic that poems for a *New Hampshire* collection were written in Vermont. It has been said that "Stopping by the Woods on a Snowy Evening" was a perfect lyrical poem.

Although he died in Boston, he is buried in the Old Burying Ground next to the First Congregational Church in Bennington. Although Frost was not born in Bennington, did not live in Bennington and did not die in Bennington, his love of the iconic First Congregational Church in Bennington caused him to be buried there.

43
FIRST STATE-FUNDED ORCHESTRA

In 1934, in the middle of the Great Depression, a group of Vermont musicians decided to create a statewide Vermont orchestra. At the center of this group was a youthful musician, Alan Carter, who had studied music abroad and who began to gather musical talents scattered around Vermont. The organizing task was enormous. With a small state population and no interstate highways or paved roads, finding talent in rural Vermont was difficult. Even more difficult was assembling an orchestra for performances and rehearsals. The initial group developed a unique strategy; they would hold concerts at various locations in the state rather than in just one place. The downside of this strategy was that the orchestra would have to travel to small gymnasiums, racetracks, armories or even outdoor hillside venues in order to perform. The early orchestras were composed of people with assorted occupations such as mechanics, lawyers, farmers and doctors.

Five years later, the 1939 New York World's Fair gave the Vermont Orchestra a big boost. The state legislature voted $1,000 for the formal formation and substance of the orchestra, including enough funds to attend the world's fair to perform and promote Vermont. As the current Vermont Symphony Orchestra (VSO) executive director Ben Cadwallader put it, "Vermont's reputation was kind of a backwater bunch of farmers in the woods. Rural. There's no culture. No kind of city life." He added, "The legislature had the wisdom to say, 'Actually, you know, let's go to the biggest stage in the world and show people how wrong they are. Yeah, we do have farms in Vermont, but Vermont's much more than just dairy cows and sheep.'"

Vermont Symphony Orchestra performing in 2019 in Chittenden. *Vermont Symphony Orchestra and vibecommercialimaging.com.*

Fortunately, the legislature continued appropriating funds for the orchestra. This funding was remarkable because it came from a relatively poor state with precious few dollars and people unemployed. The initial state funding made the Vermont Symphony Orchestra the first state-funded symphony orchestra.

Today, the Vermont Symphony Orchestra comprises essentially all professional musicians, but it has stayed true to its roots and performs all over Vermont, not just in one venue. The Vermont Symphony Orchestra now has small spinoff groups such as a bass quintet that also play around the state. The real embodiment of that theme of "music to the people" is the annual tour of the full Vermont Symphony Orchestra to about eight or nine different towns around the state during the first week of July for outdoor concerts and fireworks. As Ben Cadwallader can attest, "This state is a hub for some of the best music on our planet."

44

LARGEST ZIPPER

The sixty-eight-foot-long granite zipper is located in the city of Barre. The famous Barre quarries of granite are known worldwide. The deepest dimension granite quarry in the world is located in Barre. Hand in hand with granite production, Barre has a long history of art, including the legendary granite gravestone carvings in Barre's Hope Cemetery, which showcase the historical talent of Barre quarry carvers.

The largest zipper is located on North Main Street, Barre, Vermont. *Sue Higby/Studio Place Arts and photo by Petra Tasiopoulos.*

Therefore, it is not surprising that the creativity and civic responsibility available in Barre led to the creation of the largest zipper. The long narrow space between the Space Place Arts building and the bank required updating and a way to utilize the small area. A place to sit was needed, as was a park for locals to congregate and enjoy the small urban space.

Artists, landowners, civic-minded people, nonprofits and others came together to create an amazing park just off North Main Street (Route 302) in Barre that can be enjoyed by everyone. As best described by Sue Higby, executive director of Studio Place Arts:

The 68-foot-long zipper, commissioned by Studio Place Arts (SPA), was made by Calais VT artist Chris Miller. It was created from carved and stacked Barre gray granite. It runs along the side of the historic SPA building, also known as the historic "Nichols Block" and is "unzipped" to expose a lush perennial garden inside. The granite zipper is the artistic focal point for the small park in downtown historic Barre.

45

FIRST PERSON TO HAVE A PRIVATE U.S. POST OFFICE

Although Rudyard Kipling was born in 1865 in Bombay, India, and spent only a few years in Vermont, he produced some of his best and most famous works in Vermont.

Kipling's early life included education in England and work in British India for various newspapers. Even at a young age, he loved writing. After writing for local papers in various towns, he left India for London in 1889. He took a circuitous route to the Far East and then to the United States, where his travels started on the West Coast and ended in Boston.

Kipling ended his journey in London in 1889 and stayed two years. While in London, he met an American author, Wolcott Balestier, with whom he collaborated on a novel titled *Naulahka*. (The spelling of *Naulahka* changed later) Traveling again, he went to South Africa, New Zealand and back to India. He immediately returned to London when he heard his friend Wolcott Balestier had suddenly died. In London, on January 18, 1892, he married Wolcott's sister, Caroline "Carrie" Balestier, thus cementing the Vermont connection.

Carrie, aged twenty-nine, and Rudyard, aged twenty-six, went on their honeymoon to Japan, with a first stop in the United States that included a visit to the Balestier family home near Brattleboro, Vermont. They went on to Japan, but because of bank failures, they were forced to return to Vermont, where they rented a small cottage called Bliss Cottage on a farm near Brattleboro. Carrie was pregnant and had her first child in that cottage. Significantly, mostly during the winter of 1892, it was in this cottage that the first drawings for the famous *Jungle Book* were made.

With Bliss Cottage being small and the couple having a newborn child, they bought ten acres nearby and started building a house they called Naulakha, in honor of the name of the book he and his deceased brother-in-law had collaborated on. The Kiplings' new house, which was just across the Brattleboro line in Dummerston, brought the author "sunshine and a mind at ease." Seclusion in Vermont brought Kipling a "sane clean life," keeping him inventive and prolific.

Two firsts occurred while Kipling was in Dummerston. During his stay in Naulakha, he had several visitors. One was Arthur Conan Doyle, who brought some golf clubs. Kipling apparently liked the game so much that he became the first to invent "winter golf" by painting the golf ball red to find it in the snow. It never really caught on, but it was Kipling who was the FIRST to play the game. In the summer, he played tennis on the Naulakha tennis court, which is purported to be the first court in Vermont.

When Kipling settled down in Vermont at age twenty-eight, he was already a well-known international author, which caused problems. He didn't like his local post office because of all the commotion there when he would visit. He traveled to neighboring Brattleboro, but he didn't like the short trip from

Rudyard Kipling's house, Naulakha, in Dummerston, Vermont, circa 1905. *Library of Congress, Prints and Photographs Division.*

Dummerston. It was estimated he was receiving over two hundred letters a day, which he was told was more mail than the largest company in the area, the famous Estey Organ Company. The postmaster authorized the establishment of a special post office, the first of its kind, just for him. In 1895, his Dummerston neighbor, Anna Waite, became the postmistress, and her house served as the post office. Today, the postmark "Waite, Vermont," is prized by stamp collectors. After an unfortunate dispute with a brother-in-law, Rudyard Kipling left his beloved Vermont in 1896. In 1897, the post office was closed and never opened again.

There is no evidence that a similar post office was opened earlier anywhere else in the United States for the sole purpose of serving one person (not a corporation) and was in a private home with its own postmaster or mistress.

The Nobel Prize for Literature was established in 1901, and Rudyard Kipling became the first English-language recipient on December 10, 1907, in Stockholm. He died in 1936 at age seventy.

Naulakha is now owned by the Landmark Trust USA and is a National Historic Landmark in Dummerston. It has been beautifully restored to look almost as it looked when the Kipling was in residence writing *The Jungle Book*. It can be rented and used as sleeping quarters.

Although Kipling spent only four years in Vermont, his wife's family had been here for years. While in Naulakha, Kipling also wrote *Captain Courageous* and the first of the "Just So Stories." He also wrote the early draft of *Kim* while in Dummerston.

46

FIRST AMERICAN WOMAN TO WIN NOBEL PRIZE FOR LITERATURE

Pearl Buck was the daughter of American Presbyterian missionaries who lived in China from about 1880 to 1892. When they returned to West Virginia, they gave birth to their daughter Pearl on June 26, 1892. When Pearl was only five months old, the family returned to China, where she grew up.

In 1911, at age eighteen, Pearl returned to the United States to attend Virginia's Randolph-Macon College. After four years in America, Pearl returned to China in 1914, married John Lossing Buck in 1917 and stayed there almost another twenty years, until 1934. She then came back to the United States and never returned to the Far East.

It was during her stays in China that she finished the manuscript for her novel *The Good Earth* about rural Chinese peasant life. It was published in 1931. In 1932, she won the Pulitzer Prize for literature for *The Good Earth.* In 1938, back in the United States, she won the Nobel Prize for Literature, the first American woman to do so. The Nobel Prize was not awarded specifically for *The Good Earth* but rather for "her rich and truly epic descriptions of peasant life in China and her biographical masterpieces." Before and after its publication in 1932, she had written many other novels, short stories and nonfiction works.

For her years in the United States from 1935 to 1950, she traveled to and had a home in Pennsylvania. In 1950, she purchased property in Winhall, Vermont, near Stratton ski area. On that property, she and her three sons built a house that she used as her vacation home. Pearl Buck Drive in Winhall is named in her honor. The house was built before Stratton ski area was opened, but after Stratton was built, she could see it from her writing office. Buck's move to Vermont was based in part by meeting Arlington's Dorothy Canfield and her love of rural living, which she developed while in China. As one writer said:

> *Pearl had reared her children to be self-sufficient, insisting they needed practical skills as well as college educations (the three boys regularly spent vacations working on a plot of land she bought in Vermont, clearing the ground and mixing concrete to build a cabin in the woods which became the family summer holiday home).*

In 1969, she bought a house in the rural small town of Danby, Vermont, about thirty miles from Stratton. To put the size of Danby in perspective, the store she was operating had three stories, and it was, as she stated, the tallest building in Southern Vermont. She continued to live in Danby and died there on March 6, 1973. Her grave site in Perkasie, Bucks County, Pennsylvania, is made of Vermont granite.

Pearl S. Buck had been coming to Vermont for almost twenty-five years, nearly a quarter of her life. During her Vermont years, she wrote three autobiographies, over fifteen novels, over ten nonfiction books and over forty short stories. In 1973, she was inducted into the Women's Hall of Fame. In 1983, the U.S. Postal Service issued a five-cent stamp to recognize a lifetime of service. In 1999, she was designated a Women's History Month Honoree by the National Women's History Project. She also started the FIRST multiracial orphanage, the Welcome House, to help children born to U.S. servicemen overseas.

XI

FARMS

47

FIRST DOCUMENTED AMERICAN HORSE BREED

Justin Morgan, a schoolteacher and musician, was born on February 28, 1747, in West Springfield, Massachusetts. By 1788, at age forty-one, he had moved and settled in Vermont. Justin returned to Massachusetts in 1792 to take title of a foundation sire, Figure, to help settle a debt. Figure had been born in 1789 in West Springfield. He was about fourteen hands (fifty-six inches) high as measured to the withers. At around one thousand pounds, he was smallish by many standards.

During the period that Justin Morgan owned Figure from 1792 to 1795, he was used on neighbors' farms for tasks that required a harness such as ploughing and logging. People noticed Figure could pull heavier loads than draft horses but could, in contrast, outrun some thoroughbred horses in match races. He was a fast harness racer. Other farmers in Vermont who would own Figure over the years also noticed these unusual speed and strength characteristics.

One of Figure's other amazing abilities was to convey these diverse capabilities to his offspring through a variety of mates. Other characteristics that were imparted included good looks, balanced temperament and athleticism. Over time, the breed became known as the Morgan horse after the original owner, Justin Morgan, who died in 1798 at age fifty-one.

Figure passed away in 1821, twenty-three years after Justin Morgan died. He is buried in Tunbridge, Vermont, which is about fifteen miles from Randolph, where Justin Morgan had been a town clerk at one time.

Over time and well into the nineteenth century, Morgan horses proved to be an extremely versatile breed. They were champion harness racers, ranch horses, cutting horses, cavalry horses, work horses, plow horses and

UVM Zachariah is with farm manager Kimberly Demars in the early morning mist at the University of Vermont Morgan Horse Farm in Weyridge. The UVM prefix denotes the horse was born and bred on the UVM Morgan Horse Farm. *Author's collection.*

carriage pullers. Because of the importance of the breed, in 1857, D.C. Linsley published a book titled *Morgan Horses*, which documented the breed in a formal manner. There are other American breeds that might have come first, but Linsley's book made the Morgan the first American breed with formal documentation. In 1894, thirty-seven years after the Linsey book, the first volume of the *American Morgan Horse Register* was published by Colonel Joseph Battell, further documenting the Morgan breed.

Many accolades have been bestowed on the Morgan breed. At one time, it was the official horse of the U.S. cavalry. A commemorative stamp was issued by the U.S. government depicting the Morgan horse. Both the North and South in the Civil War favored the Morgan for its temperament under fire. General Philip Sheridan of the Union army is said to have ridden a Morgan. Ethan Allen, a Morgan horse, was one of the fastest trotters in the 1850s. As a side note, the popular trotting weathervane was based on the Ethan Allen silhouette. As further tribute to the Morgan, the U.S. Department of Agriculture commissioned the U.S. Morgan Horse Farm in Weybridge, adjacent to Middlebury, in 1907. It appears that this was the FIRST time the U.S. government tried to perpetuate and improve an American breed. The farm was originally established in 1878, but in 1951, the University of Vermont (UVM) became the farm's steward. Today, the beautiful UVM Morgan Horse Farm is open to the public and is home to over forty Morgan horses. The site is in the National Register of Historic Places.

48

FIRST COMMERCIALLY SUCCESSFUL STEEL PLOW

John Deere was born in Rutland on February 7, 1804, and the following year his family moved to Middlebury. When Deere was four years old, his father, who had been in the tailoring business, left for England and was never seen again. As a result, Deere was raised by his mother. Deere's only formal education was probably in the Vermont public school system.

At age seventeen, in 1821, Deere started to apprentice for a blacksmith in Middlebury, but about four years later he set out on his own. For the next twelve years, he was working and setting up blacksmith shops throughout Vermont. During this period, in 1827, he married Demarius Lamb and eventually had nine children in their thirty-eight-year marriage.

After thirty-three years of living and working in Vermont, bad fortune turned into good fortune. The bad fortune came in 1836 when economic hard times forced him to move west from Vermont to Grand Detour, Illinois. There Deere established a blacksmith shop, and two years later, he sent for his wife.

In Grand Detour, Deere's Vermont experiences and hard work set him on the path to greatness. Repeatedly, he found himself repairing and cleaning old wood and cast-iron plows for the prairie farmers. The light sandy soils of Vermont could be handled easily with the existing plows, but the soils of the Midwest prairielands caused problems for the plows because of fertile but thick heavy soils.

As he was a well-trained blacksmith, it didn't take Deere long to start experimenting with several designs that would allow for a self-scouring

The 1838 John Deere plow made in Grand Detour, Illinois, was on display at the Smithsonian Institution, Washington. *Library of Congress, Prints and Photograph Division, Harris and Ewing Collection.*

(cleaning) plow. His skills allowed him to experiment with various plow prototypes. One design that seemed to work had a curved polished steel blade (moldboard). By using cast steel rather than cast iron, he could polish the plow easier so sod would not stick. The polishing idea came from his Vermont experience polishing needles with sand in his family tailor shop.

After just one year in Illinois, in 1838, Deere sold three plows. In 1839, he sold ten, and in 1840, he sold forty. In 1843, growing demand prompted Deere to form a partnership with Leonard Andrus, and by 1846, they had made one thousand plows. The following year, Deere sold his interest to his partner and moved to Moline, Illinois, to take advantage of better water power and coal, which was important in the steel business. Not only was Moline a better place to build the plows, but it was better for marketing as well. Having lived in Vermont and traveled to many farms, he knew the market. Moline was on the Mississippi River, which allowed Deere to get his plows to market easier. Today, Moline, Illinois, is one of the famous Quad

Cities, with Iowa located across the river. Iowa had just become a state and was growing rapidly in the agricultural arena.

In 1858, Deere took his son Charles into partnership, and in 1863, his son-in-law Stephen H. Veille joined the firm. In 1868, he incorporated Deere and Company. As time went on, Deere produced a variety of agricultural equipment, including cultivators and more.

John Deere passed away on May 17, 1886, at age eighty-two. Deere had also been active in local government, civic groups and the Congregational Church.

Deere's thirty-three years in Vermont served him well. He learned the blacksmithing trade, how to run a blacksmith business and how to be independent and self-sufficient—plus he had become familiar with the agricultural market needs.

49

LARGEST MAPLE SUGAR PRODUCER

Vermont has consistently led the United States in the production of maple syrup. In 2019, Vermont produced 2,070,000 gallons, with the number two producer, New York, producing 820,000 gallons and number three, Maine, producing 580,000 gallons. Vermont's production was about 48 percent of the total U.S. production. Vermont's total production was two and a half times that of the second producer, New York.

Several factors contribute to this leadership. First, Vermont has a high percentage of sugar maples, which are the preferred tree for sap. Although red, black silver and ash leaf maples produce sap, the sugar content of the sugar maple at 2 percent is about double the 1 percent content of the other maple species. Vermont has a high sugar maple population because in the late 1800s and early 1900s, many areas of Vermont were 70 to 80 percent deforested due to lumbering and sheep farming. Lumbering cut many of the soft woods such as pines, which resulted in a soil composition that favored the regrowth of the sugar maples.

Second, Vermont has favorable weather for sap production. Ideal temperatures for sap production are 20°F at night and 40°F in the day. A large portion of Vermont has this weather pattern in late March and early April. In 2019, the Vermont sap season was thirty-four days; New York's was thirty-two days, and Maine had thirty-one.

Thirdly, economics favor Vermont. Not only are there a large number of sugar maple trees but they also are concentrated. Collecting sap from dispersed maple trees is not as efficient as gathering from trees side by side.

Sap gathering from sugar maple trees, circa 1940. *Library of Congress, Prints and Photograph Division, FSA/OWI Collection.*

Even the new tube systems are more economical if trees are close together. Vermont has many sugar bushes, which are essentially stands or groves of sugar maples. These sugar bushes make it economical to build a sugar shack nearby, where sap can be evaporated to get maple sugar. Sugar maples are not as fast growing as pines and other tree species. Although some research into tapping into saplings is being explored, it is not easy for other producing areas to start large maple farms to start tapping quickly. Sugar maples are usually tapped at thirty to forty years.

Fourth, tapping has traditionally been very labor intensive. Tap holes have to be drilled, taps inserted, buckets hung and so forth. The sap-filled buckets are emptied into larger containers and taken to the sugar house. Vermont's preponderance of small family farms means family members, including children, were available. To make one gallon of pure maple syrup, twenty to forty gallons of sap are required. If there are one to three taps per tree and each tree produces nine to thirteen gallons per season, that translates roughly to needing over two trees per gallon of maple syrup per season. Based on U.S. Department of Agriculture data, Vermont would need to tap around four million trees to get two million gallons of maple syrup. Today's tube systems, which run tubes between trees to collect sap continuously, still have to be installed, maintained, cleaned, inspected and repaired. The sap season is also an ideal time in agricultural Vermont for labor ability, as spring planting has not yet occurred and winter repairs on machinery are generally over.

Fifth, Vermont as a state has maintained a high-quality product. Grading systems for maple syrup have varied between states and other countries and continue to change. However, Vermont has had a slightly higher standard of product density—almost 1 percent more sugar and less water compared to some other U.S. grades. As grading systems have changed, this reputation continues with the public perception of genuine Vermont maple syrup.

Sixth, Vermont has kept up with technology and explored ways to improve efficiencies. Universities are involved, including the University of Vermont. The tube system was invented in 1959 and vastly improved in the 1970s. Later developments include vacuum pumps to speed the flow of sap.

50
MOST CHEESEMAKERS PER CAPITA

Vermont has 66 cheesemakers and a population of about 626,000 people. That equates to about 10.5 cheesemakers for every 100,000 people. As a comparison, Wisconsin has the largest cheese production with about 89 cheesemakers and 5.8 million people. That is 1.5 cheesemakers per 100,000 people. The next-largest cheese producer is California, with approximately 50 cheesemakers and a population of about 39.5 million. California has only .2 cheesemakers for every 100,000 people.

Cheesemakers refers to a company or organizations producing cheese, not the individual cheesemaker. For instance, a company may have five individual cheesemakers, but the company counts as one. Counting the number of actual producers is difficult, but Vermont is so far ahead that even some changes in the number of cheesemakers would not change the ratio of cheesemakers per capita.

Several key factors may contribute to Vermont having a disproportionate number of cheesemakers per capita. Vermont's topography is hilly and lends itself to grazing for goats, sheep, cows, llamas and alpacas. From the establishment of Vermont as a state in 1791, our dairy farms have tended to be smaller in nature. The New Hampshire land grants that created Vermont were small by design, to give individuals the ability to own and work their own land. Given the small nature of our dairy farms and the price competitiveness of the dairy business, Vermont farmers have found ways to add value to pure milk by also making cheese. Varied topography lends itself to different varieties of cheeses, which means individual small companies are able to compete.

Vermont cheese sculpture on display at the Washington County fair. *Author's collection.*

FIRST STATE DAIRY ASSOCIATION

The first state dairyman association was established on October 27, 1869. The group has evolved into the Vermont Dairy Industry Association. The association recognizes that the industry goes beyond dairymen and includes many key players like farmers, processors, educators, marketing and regulatory personnel.

XII

TRANSPORTATION

51

FIRST CANAL USED CONTINUOUSLY FOR INDUSTRIAL PURPOSES

In Bellows Falls, on the Connecticut River, a historic marker erected by the Vermont Department of Historic Preservation reads, "Here first Canal in United States was built in 1802." By their very nature, historic markers, because of space restraints, are limited by the number of words that can be used. Merriam-Webster dictionary defines the term *canal* as "an artificial waterway for navigation, draining or irrigating land." By using that definition, the first canal could have been thousands of years ago, when an irrigation ditch was built by Native Americans. However, modern general usage of the word would tend to call an irrigation canal a ditch, sluiceway or raceway rather than a canal. Canal generally implies commercial or industrial usage.

Dan Axtell did some good research to identify eleven U.S. canals other than the Bellows Falls Canal that claim some form of canal first: Cut River (Massachusetts, 1636), Mother Brook (Massachusetts, 1639), the Neck Diged Through (New York, 1730), Schuylkill and Susquehanna (Pennsylvania, 1762), James River (Virginia, 1789), Susquehanna (Maryland, 1783), Patowmack (Virginia, 1802), South Hadley (Massachusetts, 1794), Little Falls (New York, 1795), Conewago (Pennsylvania, 1797) and Old Santee (South Carolina, 1793).

None of those eleven canals was both built for navigation and has also been in continuous use either for navigation or other industrial uses. The Bellows Falls Canal was built for navigation and is still in use to supply

Bellows Falls Canal around 1907. *Library of Congress, Prints and Photographs Division.*

power and has operated continuously. Using the modern definition, built for navigation, the Bellows Falls Canal is the first canal used continuously for industrial purposes. The Bellows Falls Canal is still alive and well and can be seen year-round.

52

FIRST COAST-TO-COAST ROAD TRIP

This adventure could have also been called the FIRST cross-country automobile race, since two other cars were trying to catch and beat him to New York from the West Coast. The thrilling story of Horatio Nelson Jackson has been immortalized in a Ken Burns movie, *Horatio's Drive,* starring Tom Hanks as Jackson. The Smithsonian National Museum of American History in Washington also constructed an exhibit featuring the original Winton touring car, the Vermont, to recognize Nelson's amazing first.

Horatio Nelson Jackson was born in Toronto, Canada, on March 25, 1872, to American parents, but he ended up living in Vermont and graduating from the University of Vermont. He became a physician and a businessman as well as an automobile enthusiast. After practicing medicine in Brattleboro and Burlington, he was forced to give up his profession due to health issues.

At age thirty-one, Jackson was married and no longer practicing medicine. While visiting San Francisco, Nelson and his wife had been taking driving lessons, when he became convinced that the automobile was not a passing fad. He became a guest at the University Club in San Francisco on May 18, 1903.

At the University Club, a fifty-dollar wager was offered to him betting that he could not drive an automobile from San Francisco to New York. This trip had never been done before. At the time of the wager, he did not own a car and had no maps, little driving experience and no mechanical experience. After giving her blessing, his wife returned to Vermont via train, and his adventure began.

Starting immediately, Jackson purchased a used 1903 Winton touring car and gathered a range of supplies, such as a block and tackle, spare parts, pistols, a camera and so forth. Because of his lack of mechanical experience, he then asked a young mechanic and chauffeur, Sewall K. Crocker, to join him as backup driver and mechanic. He named the car the Vermont. On May 23, 1903, Crocker and Jackson set out in a car that had no top and no windshield. They also knew that there were very few paved roads between San Francisco and New York except in the cities.

Alexander Winton, whose company manufactured the Vermont, had tried the same trip two years prior but failed because the deserts of Nevada and Utah had no paved roads. He was forced to quit. Jackson, on the other hand, decided to take the northern route to avoid these desert pitfalls as well as some Rocky Mountain obstacles.

The journey began with a blown tire on the first day. At times, they wound rope around the tire rims to act as tires. With no paved roads, no gas stations, no GPS, no maps, no restaurants, no FedEx or UPS to overnight spare

Horatio Nelson Jackson is shown in his 1903 Winton he named the Vermont. *University of Vermont Special Collections.*

parts from the factory, minor mishaps on this journey became disastrous and continuous. Receiving wrong directions caused them once to go over a hundred miles out of their way. Other problems were lost eyeglasses and leaks causing fuel and oil to be lost. Once, a cowboy on horseback needed to tow the car. At one time, a forty-five-mile bicycle trip was made to get more gasoline. Burned-out wheel bearings and lost money added to their woes. Soothing these mishaps was their dog, Bud, which they had acquired and outfitted with goggles.

Despite these many problems, Jackson, in the Vermont, arrived in New York on July 26, 1903. This was exactly sixty-three days, twelve hours and thirty minutes after he had started. Although two other cars were trying to beat Jackson and were better financially backed, they lost, and the Vermont finished first.

Jackson's travels had been covered coast-to-coast by the press, with thousands coming out to meet him and see the Vermont. This journey created a major push for the development of more paved roads, the establishment of service stations and the production of better road maps. This feat has been honored with an exhibit at the Smithsonian National Museum of American History, and a U.S. postage stamp featuring the Vermont was issued.

Jackson himself was no one-hit wonder. Living in Burlington, Vermont, with his wife and Bud, he went on to be a successful businessman. Although older, he served in World War I as a captain in the Medical Corps and earned a Distinguished Service Cross for heroism in France.

53
FIRST GLOBE FACTORY

James Wilson, a self-made man, was born in Londonderry, New Hampshire, on March 15, 1763. He became a farmer and blacksmith, and at age thirty-two, in 1795, he moved to Vermont, which had become the fourteenth state only four years earlier in 1791.

Wilson's home was in rural Bradford, Orange County, which is on the Connecticut River about twenty-five miles north of Norwich. Sometime in the late 1790s, when Wilson was about thirty-five years old, he had a life-changing experience. He visited Dartmouth College and was captivated by a pair of English-made terrestrial and celestial globes. He was fascinated by the globes and decided that he could make better ones in the United States. He would need to overcome major problems because he knew nothing about engraving, geography or astronomy.

To learn geography and astronomy, he bought an *Encyclopedia Britannica* from a neighbor in Vermont. To learn the skill of engraving, he went on foot to see Amos Doolittle in Connecticut, who had engraved two maps in Jedediah Morse's 1784 *Geography Made Easy*. Wilson learned from Doolittle the basics of engraving on copper and then walked back to Bradford.

Wilson was a self-made man when he started out in the globe business in Vermont. He had learned the blacksmith business; therefore, he did nearly everything himself. He made his own tools, lathes, presses, ink, glue and varnish. He designed all of his own maps with some advice from Jedediah Morse (1761–1826), who was known as the "father of American geography."

This original James A. Wilson globe is part of the Bennington Museum collection. *Bennington Museum.*

He started to produce globes in his blacksmith shop, which became the first "globe manufactory." Luckily, three of his children—Samuel, John and David—were teenagers and anxious to help. James Wilson would, in his lifetime, have fourteen children. Apparently, his first globe sold was in 1810. Records are scarce, but he may have sold a few globes prior to 1810. One of his first models was solid wood. Shortly after that first globe sale, Wilson sold over twenty-five more. He produced the first "perfected" artificial globe in 1811. Besides the globes, he also had other commercial engraving businesses. These businesses helped support him while his globe business grew.

Around 1815, he expanded his globe business to Albany, New York, which represented a bigger market. He opened an Albany "manufactory" at 110 Washington Street under the title James Wilson & Sons. The Albany manufactory was essentially run by his sons, but the main factory was kept in Bradford.

James would also go on to develop and sell planetariums. His globes came in at least three sizes—thirteen, nine and three inches—and he had both terrestrial, which showed earth points, and celestial, which showed the stars' locations. James Wilson died at age ninety-two. Of his ninety-two years, he lived in Vermont for almost fifty-nine years and ran his business from his Bradford globe factory.

James Wilson's home site in Bradford is marked with a Vermont Division of Historic Preservation marker. There was a large handmade globe made in St. Albans in 1811, but credit for the first perfected globe and globe factory in the United States goes to James Wilson.

54

FIRST SUCCESSFUL FAST MAIL DELIVERY BY HORSE

William Hepburn Russell was born in Burlington in 1812. His father was William Eaton Russell, who died in Burlington on January 14, 1814, as a result of the War of 1812. William H. Russell had three sisters, all of whom were born in Vermont: Emeline Marcia Russell (1806–1891), Adeline Russell (1808–1809) and Adeline Elizabeth "Adela" Russell (1811–1839). His eldest sister, Emeline, lived to be eighty-five years old.

William H. Russell's mother married Oliver Bangs in 1816 and moved the family to western Missouri. He was four years old; his eldest sister was ten, and his other sister was five. It's not known exactly where in western Missouri they lived. His stepfather had acquired work at an Iowa Indian Agency. Little is known about Oliver Bangs, but presumably he also had some experience or background in Vermont or at least the North Country.

William H. Russell left home in 1824, at age twelve, to work in Liberty, Missouri. His sister Emeline Marcia Russell married Dudley Avery and delivered her first child in 1824, when she was eighteen. William H. Russell was close to his Vermont family and influences from 1812 until at least 1824, or more than twelve years.

After leaving home at twelve, William H. Russell had a variety of jobs and ventures prior to starting the Pony Express. While still in his teens, Russell went to work as a general store clerk in Liberty, which is in western Missouri, probably still near his family. Two years later, in 1830, he worked at a mercantile firm and learned the wholesale business. In 1835, at age twenty-three, he married the daughter of a Baptist minister, which later would help

This is a wood engraving rendering of a Pony Express rider passing a crew putting up a telegraph line. *Library of Congress, Prints and Photographs Division.*

with his social standing. In 1840, he organized a company and met his future partner in the Pony Express, William B. Waddell. In 1844, he opened a general store, which he expanded to shipping goods west to New Mexico. He then joined the firm of Waddell, Ramsey and & Co., and by 1848, he was successful enough to buy a twenty-room mansion in Lexington, Missouri. He became involved with another venture, the military freight business.

In 1852, Russell partnered again with Waddell, and by 1854, he was freighting military supplies to Santa Fe. His venture with Waddell became the largest freighting company in western Missouri. When the gold rush came to Colorado, Russell transported passengers, mail, freight and gold to Pikes Peak and bought the company that had the postal contract between St. Joseph, Missouri, and Salt Lake City. The postal contract was to run out in November 1860. The year before, in 1859, Alexander Majors, William B. Waddell and William Hepburn Russell partnered to form Central Overland California & Pikes Peak Express Company (COC and PP) with hopes of carrying mail to California.

On January 27, 1860, Russell wrote his son, "Have determined to establish a Pony Express to Sacramento, California commencing 3rd April 1860. Time, 10 days." Under a charter from Kansas and using horses, not traditional stagecoaches, a fast mail service was established between St. Joseph, Missouri, and Sacramento, California.

By most accounts, although there were three founders associated with the Pony Express, the driving force had been Russell. Apparently, he was a man of great gentility and given to formal speech and manner. According to the *Encyclopedia Britannica*, he played "a vital role as its visionary and its liaison with government officials as well as business community."

The Pony Express would operate from April 3, 1860, to October 24, 1861, only about nineteen months. The Civil War had come, and the telegraph was by far the fastest way to get messages west. The COC and PP Express assets were sold to a Benjamin Hollady, who, in November 1866, sold the assets to Wells Fargo. One of the partners of Wells Fargo was Henry Wells, who was born in Thetford, Vermont, in 1805. He was seven years older than William Russell.

Although the Pony Express operated for only nineteen months, it is embedded in the folklore of the old West. In 1860, there were over 180 stations along the 1,900-mile route and more than 400 horses. It took ten days for the first westbound trip to go from St. Joseph, Missouri, to Sacramento, California.

Most of the Pony Express horses were about 14.2 hands. Since a pony is defined in many cases as being smaller than 14.2 hands, most of the horses were on the small side, which made the moniker appropriate. The somewhat smaller Morgan horses were also used, mainly in the more eastern sections of the Pony Express route. Each rider rode about seventy-five miles.

A three-cent commemorative U.S. postal stamp memorialized this romantic part of American folklore. William Hepburn Russell died on September 10, 1872, in Missouri eleven years after the Pony Express stopped operating.

55
FIRST REJECTION OF A MAJOR WPA PROJECT

In the early 1930s, there was a proposal to build a Green Mountain Parkway (GMP) that would weave north for about 260 miles from the Massachusetts border to the Canadian border, generally along the spine of Vermont's Green Mountains. It was to be similar to the Skyline Drive in Virginia.

Mainly funded by the federal government as part of the Depression-era New Deal, the parkway would have had significant impact on Vermont had it been built. Some said the effect would be positive, and others said it would be negative.

The Federal Works Progress Administration (WPA) was part of the broad New Deal under President Franklin Delano Roosevelt. (The WPA was later renamed the Work Projects Administration.) The WPA was signed into law on May 6, 1935. A main purpose of the WPA was to provide jobs through construction of roads and other public works projects. On March 3, 1936, ten months after the law was signed, Vermont voters at town meetings rejected the parkway proposal by defeating a bond issue that would pay for funding Vermont's small share of the projects cost.

To put this project in context, in the early 1930s, during the middle of the Great Depression, there were an estimated twelve thousand Vermonters on relief. As a federal program essentially handing out free money, the parkway would have created about six to eight thousand jobs. Vermont would be required to pay only $500,000 to buy rights of way. The federal government would be responsible for the remaining $18 million.

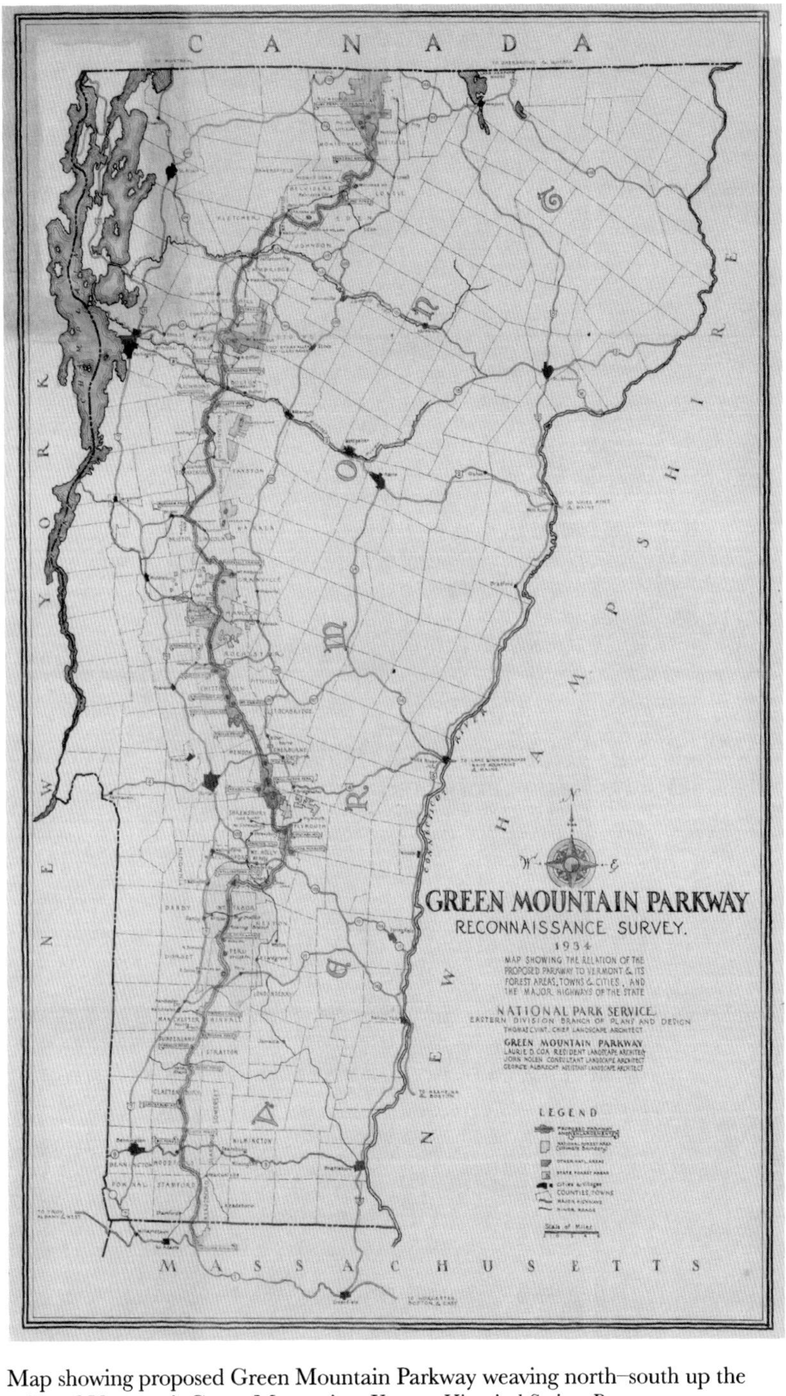

Map showing proposed Green Mountain Parkway weaving north–south up the spine of Vermont's Green Mountains. *Vermont Historical Society, Barre.*

Towns and cities throughout the United States were willing to accept federal money to build a wide variety of projects such as golf courses, bridges, roads, public buildings, schools and hospitals. In essence, free money was being offered for construction of public conveniences. During the first ten months of the WPA, there is no evidence of any significant project being rejected by a statewide vote other than Vermont's GMP.

Proponents and opponents of the GMP raised issues that would have forever affected the state. Opponents said the GMP would prevent Vermont from becoming a tourist attraction because it would no longer be able to advertise "Visit Unspoiled Vermont." Tourism was becoming as important as dairy farming and quarrying. Opponents claimed that although the federal money being offered was extremely generous for construction, Vermonters would need to pay for highway maintenance for the next hundred years. Vermont was a very poor state. Opposition also came from Southern Vermont towns that were concerned that the highway would take tourists directly to northern towns, thereby bypassing their towns. Opponents also said that federal intrusion and control of local government would end Vermont's independence and self-reliance. Large tracts of land would fall under federal control. Right or wrong, opponents said the GMP would be an eyesore, as it would destroy the ridge line. Some Vermonters simply didn't like the idea of making "Vermont like the rest of the country." Another issue was the width of the right of way and how much it would scar the mountains. At one point, opponents were talking about needing to resettle thirteen thousand people. Opponents said the parkway would split the state into east and west.

On the other hand, proponents pointed out that in 1929, the Vermont economy was getting significant revenue from the important recreation industry. Proponents said the GMP, which was billed as a recreation project, would open the Green Mountains for more recreation and tourists. The Green Mountain National Forest had been established in 1932 to open the forest to recreation and preserve it.

The parkway proposal was gathering opinions from outside of Vermont. The *Boston Herald* and the *New York Times* were writing commentary. People such as noted landscape designer Frederick Law Olmsted Jr. were voicing opinions. Proponents were mailing brochures and information to over one hundred newspapers. Even some federal officials were expressing varying opinions.

The actual voting process was unique. The state had been working on the proposal for three years, starting with the National Industrial Recovery

Act, which was declared unconstitutional in 1935. The Vermont legislature actually voted in favor of the GMP, but the legislators said they would agree with the public's wishes. Since there was not a pure referendum law in Vermont, a vote was set up for Town Meeting Day, March 3, 1936. The actual ballot question was when to start construction of the highway. Voters had two starting date choices: April 1, 1936, or April 1, 1941. The results of the votes were:

1936 start	30,897 votes
1941 start	42,318 votes

The later date won, which essentially killed the project. The Vermont legislature formally killed the project in 1937 by passing Act 243. In that year, the Writers' Project of the Public Works Administration indicated that, in effect, "in 1936 Vermont gained national notice by declining the Green Mountain Parkway." As quoted in *The Vermont Way*, the highly respected Frank Bryan, political science professor emeritus at UVM, stated the defeat of the GMP was "the MOST democratic expression of environmental consciousness in American history, mythic in its defiance and radical in its implications—a Vermont that is green and rebellious."

56

FIRST SAFETY ELEVATOR

Elisha Otis did not invent the elevator, but he did invent the safety elevator by creating a mechanism that would stop an elevator from going into a free fall if the cables broke.

Otis was born on August 3, 1811, in rural Halifax, Vermont, which is about twenty miles west of Brattleboro in southeast Vermont. Otis was raised on his parents' successful farm but spent most of his time in blacksmith

A rendering of Elisha Otis in 1854 demonstrating that his safety elevator would not free fall even if the cable is cut. *Wiki Commons.*

shops because he loved to invent and tinker. At the time, there were plenty of blacksmith shops to explore in Vermont.

After nineteen years in Vermont, he grew restless and left the state. He ended up working as a carpenter and wagon hauler in Troy, New York, just outside Albany. Shortly after his marriage in 1834 at age twenty-three, he moved back to the Brattleboro region due to ill health. In Vermont, he built a gristmill with his own designs and subsequently turned the gristmill into a sawmill. Apparently, that sawmill was not successful, because in 1845 he moved back to Albany.

At age thirty-four, after trying several jobs in Albany, he moved to Yonkers, outside New York City, then to Jersey City, also outside New York City. Finally, in Jersey City he used wagon parts to create the famous patented braking systems for elevators. By making it safe to transport people vertically, Otis had opened up the world to high-rise buildings such as skyscrapers.

Otis died at the young age of forty-nine on April 8, 1861. Over half of Otis's life was spent in Vermont, where he became familiar with mechanical devices, wagons, blacksmith shops and wagon braking devices.

XIII

NONPROFITS

57

OLDEST SON OF ABRAHAM LINCOLN

Friends of Hildene Inc. is a nonprofit organization that operates Hildene, the Lincoln Family Home, in Manchester. Robert Todd Lincoln was born in Springfield, Illinois, in 1843, and there he spent his youth. He was the first born of four children, all boys, to President Abraham Lincoln. He would be the only child of Abraham Lincoln to live to maturity. In 1860, he matriculated at Harvard and graduated in 1864. While Lincoln was at Harvard, the Civil War broke out in 1861. In 1864, Robert's mother, Mary Todd Lincoln, decided to escape from the war in Washington and traveled to the Equinox House in Manchester for a brief visit. She brought her son Robert Todd Lincoln along with her.

After the Civil War, Robert Todd Lincoln became a successful lawyer and the secretary of war under two administrations. He also became the minister plenipotentiary and envoy extraordinary to the Court of St. James. Lincoln held the latter position from 1889 to 1893, which made him the last person to hold that position. The minister position then became an ambassador's position.

Lincoln went on to be president of the Pullman Palace Car Company in Chicago, which was the world's largest manufacturer of its time. Using funds he made from Pullman, he decided to build his family home. The first son of President Lincoln could have built almost anywhere, but he chose Manchester, as he had always fondly remembered visiting the area.

His home, the Lincoln Family Home, is now the magnificent Hildene in Manchester. The main house rests on 412 acres and has been occupied by

Robert Todd Lincoln's Hildene, the Lincoln Family Home, in Manchester. *Friends of Hildene Inc.*

only Lincolns since 1905, when Robert Todd Lincoln moved in. Robert died at Hildene in 1926, and the last Lincoln to reside there was Mary "Peggy" Lincoln Beckwith, who passed away in 1975 in Rutland, Vermont. One of Robert Todd Lincoln's three grandchildren, Robert Todd Lincoln Beckwith, died on December 24, 1985, thus being the LAST of President Abraham Lincoln's direct descendants.

58

FIRST BOY SCOUT TROOP

In 1907, William Foster Milne, who was born on September 23, 1885, in Aberdeen, Scotland, immigrated to the United States as a twenty-two-year-old stonecutter (carver). He was drawn to Barre by the booming granite business located there.

In 1908, Sir Baden-Powell formally established the Boy Scout Association in Britain. In 1909, Milne returned to Scotland and came back to Barre with Scouting materials. He was enthusiastic about the Scouting movement started by Baden-Powell. That year, he discovered a small organized group of boys in Barre who were members of the Boys Brigade. This group mainly performed drills and marching activities. They met at Barre's First Baptist Church. Milne suggested an alternative to the normal routines that were part of the Boys Brigade. The Boys Brigade movement had been active in England as far back as 1885. His proposal was simple: restructure into a new Boy Scout Club. This group was the first Boy Scout troop in the United States. The troop learned the diversity of the Boy Scouts by learning first aid, new outdoor skills and the art of being helpful to others. Milne held a meeting on October 24, 1909, and they voted to become the Boy Scout Club (Troop No. 1.) This group was modeled after the British Boy Scout Association but had its own flexibility.

The Boy Scouts of America would not be incorporated until the following year, February 8, 1910. Later in 1910, Barre's Troop No. 1 joined the Boy Scouts of America. It became the first troop to join the Boy Scouts of America. The Boy Scouts of America had been formally founded by W.D. Boyce

This early image shows William F. Milne (*right*), America's First Scoutmaster, with two other Scouts in Barre. *Barre Boy Scout Collection (BHC 11) Barre History Collection, Vermont Historical Society, Barre.*

on February 8, 1910, incorporating as the Boy Scouts of America. At the time of their incorporation, the Boy Scouts of America did not hold a congressional charter.

Like some other firsts, there are other claims of being the first Boy Scout troop in the United States. Many records have been lost, and there are issues of definition. However, there is strong original documentation that supports the Barre troop claims. The YMCA became the facilitator for the Boy Scouts of America as it expanded. YMCA already had camps, so it allowed troops to sign up to use these camps. On October 10, 1910, the YMCA state secretary wrote to William Milne asking for photographs of his troop, "inasmuch as they are the first troop organized in America."

It was during July of that summer that the Barre troop signed on to the Boys Scouts of America at the YMCA Camp Abenaki in North Hero, Vermont.

On February 11, 1912, Sir Francis Vane, the Grand Scout Master of the British Division of World Scouts wrote to William Milne and said, "I welcome the support of the FIRST Scoutmaster in America." Francis Vane would eventually become leader of the British Boy Scout Association.

An article in the *Barre Daily Times* of November 11, 1910, stated, "A recent letter from the national movement stated that, so far as the records show, the Barre Boy Scouts were the first organized in the United States, Springfield, Mass. being second."

Sadly, the FIRST Scoutmaster in America died on February 29, 1920, at the young age of thirty-four.

As a side note, the Honorable Governor Deane C. Davis, who was governor from 1969 to 1973, was an early "junior" member of Barre's Troop No. 1. Since Troop No. 1 was operating independently from the British Boy Scout Association, it had the flexibility to accept Scouts at the age of nine. The Boy Scouts of America later imposed twelve years as the minimum age to join.

There is a memorial to Barre Troop No. 1 in front of the First Baptist Church in Barre indicating the church was "the home of the first Boy Scout Troop in America." In 2018, a beautiful granite statue of a Boy Scout was dedicated in Barre.

FIRST ART DIRECTOR OF *BOY'S LIFE*: NORMAN ROCKWELL

Norman Rockwell, the iconic American illustrator, was born in 1894 in New York City. After going to various art schools, he was hired in 1912 as a staff artist at *Boy's Life* magazine, the official magazine of the Boy Scouts of America. The next year, at age eighteen, he was appointed as *Boy's Life*'s first art director. Although he was at the magazine for only five years, his association with the Boy Scouts of America would continue for over sixty-four years, the longest association of his career. In that period, he created an amazing 471 images for the Boy Scouts. At the age of eighty-two, Rockwell produced his last Boy Scouts illustration. It was for a calendar and titled *The Spirit of '76*. He died at age eighty-four.

Norman Rockwell made his home in Arlington from 1939 to 1952. Some of his most memorable illustrations, including some for the Boy Scouts of America, were painted while in Arlington. His paintings reflected small-town rural America. Rockwell's most famous wartime paintings, *The Four Freedoms*, were done in Arlington to raise money for war bonds during World War II.

59

FIRST NONSECTARIAN ORGANIZATION FOR GIRLS

The first Boy Scout troop was formed in 1909 in Barre, and the Boy Scouting movement was becoming popular in Vermont. Unfortunately, when Thetford, in the summer of 1910, was preparing for its 150th anniversary celebration the following year, there was no group the girls in town could join to help with the celebrations. They wanted to enjoy the same activities that the boys now had. Thetford is in rural agricultural Orange County on the Connecticut River.

The pageant's organizer, thirty-year-old William Chauncey Langdon, was sympathetic to the girls who wanted a similar group to the Boy Scouts. Langdon, who was a consultant at Russell Sage Foundation, had been brought in to direct the pageant. He approached Mrs. Charles H. Farnsworth, who was on the organizing committee, to discuss if something could be done to help the girls. Mrs. Farnsworth and her professor husband had recently founded in 1909 a camp for girls named Camp Hanoum. Based on what the Thetford girls had desired, both Langdon and Farnsworth approached Dr. Luther Halsey Gulick and his wife, Charlotte, about organizing a national group for girls. Langdon knew Dr. Gulick because Langdon was in the Department of Child Hygiene at Russell Sage Foundation that Dr. Gulick headed. Charlotte was born in nearby Hanover, New Hampshire, on the other side of the Connecticut River, about twenty miles from Thetford. Additionally, Dr. Gulick's brother was married to Mrs. Farnsworth's

U.S. commemorative stamp honoring the fiftieth anniversary of the Camp Fire Girls. The name *Camp Fire Girls* was first given to a group of girls in Thetford. *Author's collection.*

husband's sister and operated Camp Aloha in Fairlee, Vermont, near Thetford. They all knew each other well and had Vermont connections.

In 1910, with Dr. Gulick's encouragement, Langdon organized the Thetford girls and named the group Camp Fire Girls. It was the FIRST time a group of girls had been called Camp Fire Girls. Langdon also gave the Camp Fire Girls the ranks of Wood Gatherers, Fire Makers and Torch Bearers. These ranks were used for decades.

In turn, Gulick and his wife, Charlotte, approached many of his friends to support a group for girls. Gulick and his wife had been running a camp for girls in Maine. Gulick, a born organizer, merged the Thetford Camp Fire Girls and the Maine group and formally incorporated the Camp Fire Girls in Washington as a national organization on March 17, 1912.

As a nonprofit nonsectarian service organization for girls, Camp Fire Girls went on to celebrate its fiftieth anniversary in 1960. Fifteen years later, in 1974, membership had grown to 274,000. The growth is remarkable considering its small start in Thetford, Vermont.

Ironically, Camp Hanoum, founded by the Farnsworths, who were active in the founding of the Camp Fire Girls, later became Camp Farnsworth. In 1959, the land was sold to the Girl Scouts. It is still operating today.

60

FIRST ROTARY CLUB

Paul Harris was born just after the Civil War in Racine, Wisconsin, in 1868. Because there were family financial problems, Paul was sent at age three to live with his grandparents in Wallingford, just south of Rutland. The one-room primary school he attended is on Main Street, Route 7, in downtown Wallingford and is now where the local Rotary meets.

Known as a rascal, Paul attended secondary schools in nearby Rutland. He then attended Black River Academy in Ludlow but was expelled after only a few weeks. Calvin Coolidge, who was four years younger, would also attend Black River Academy. Harris managed to graduate from Vermont Military Academy, now the Vermont Academy in Saxtons River. In 1885, Paul went to the University of Vermont. Again, he ran into troubles and was expelled. His grandfather arranged for a private tutor, and Paul was able to attend Princeton University. Unfortunately, his time at Princeton was less than a year because of the passing of his grandfather in 1888.

After working at the Sheldon Marble Company in West Rutland, he moved west to Des Moines to work for a law firm. He matriculated at the University of Iowa and graduated in 1891 at the age of twenty-three. For the next five years, he held a variety of jobs, including being a cowboy and a marble and granite salesman. He then practiced law in Chicago.

Paul Harris remembered the camaraderie of meeting people of many professions in Vermont. In 1905, he formed a club to have fellowship with people of different professions. Many people he knew were from small towns like Rutland. He called the club Rotary because they would rotate among different businesses for their meetings. He had formed the first service club. It had no restrictions on religion or politics. Today, the Rotary Foundation has the largest privately funded international scholarship program.

Paul Harris was also active in other nonprofit service ventures. He was the first chairman of the board of the National Easter Seal Society for Crippled Children and Adults in the United States. He was given many awards for his philanthropic efforts, ironically including an honorary bachelor of arts degree and doctor of law degree from the University of Vermont.

XIV

POTPOURRI

61

FIRST MICROPHOTOGRAPH OF ICE CRYSTALS

Born on February 9, 1865, near Burlington in rural Jericho, Wilson Bentley continued living on his family dairy farm for his entire life. The reference to him later in life as the "Snowflake Man" understates the scientific contributions he made during his life, as his accomplishments went beyond snowflakes.

He became interested in snow crystals in his teenage years. After being home-schooled, he finally attended a formal school at age fourteen. His scientific curiosity caused him to be fascinated at age fifteen with an old microscope owned by his mother. The long, harsh Vermont winters seemed to have been one of the influences in developing his interest in snowflakes. He made hundreds of sketches of snowflakes while looking at them in the microscope.

After studying ice crystals and other objects under the microscope for about two more years, he convinced his parents to buy a bellows-style camera that could take pictures through a microscope. Although he had little knowledge of photography, he experimented with the combination of a camera and a microscope. By experimenting, he was able to create detailed images by using a large f-stop. Less than a month before his twentieth birthday, on January 15, 1885, he obtained the first successful photomicrograph of an ice crystal.

Bentley continued working on the family farm for the next thirteen years. During that time, he obtained over four hundred more photomicrographs of ice crystals. In 1898, when Bentley was thirty-three, *Popular Scientific*

Wilson "Snowflake" Bentley on his farm, pictured here sometime before 1931. *Wikimedia Commons. Public domain.*

Monthly published his first article. His writings were a wonderful combination of science and poetry. The article was a success and propelled him to a career as a scientist, writer and publisher.

Over the next ten years, he was not limited to taking images of snowflakes. He also photographed and analyzed raindrops and dew. He expanded the snowflake analysis by concluding that different geographic locations of storms produced their own type of ice crystals. His work on raindrops also produced a way to measure the size of raindrops. He was the FIRST American to record raindrop sizes. From his work, he concluded that different-sized storms produced different-sized raindrops. Another conclusion from his work was that rain could be from melting ice/snow or a process that involved no ice or snow. This last conclusion on the origins of rain is still in many ways accepted today. In summary, it has been said that Bentley should be called America's first cloud physicist.

Throughout his life of experimentation, writing and photographing, he worked on his family dairy farm. Although small in stature, around five feet tall and maybe under 125 pounds, he was muscular. He never married. He played the piano, clarinet and other instruments. Although some describe him as introverted, he had a sense of humor and entertained locals with his musical band and speeches.

Bentley died of pneumonia in Jericho on December 23, 1931. His accomplishments are enormous, and unfortunately, many of these accomplishments were only recognized after his death. He had been published in major magazines such as *Life*, *Popular Mechanics*, *National Geographic* and the *New York Times Magazine.* He took over 5,381 photomicrographs, almost all with the same camera. His works are used in university science classes throughout the world. Snowflake Bentley's writings have led to the famous simple conclusion: no two snowflakes are the same.

The Bentley home in Jericho was added to the National Register of Historic Places in 1980. The Jericho Historical Society operates the wonderful official Snowflake Bentley website.

62

FIRST PLATFORM SCALE

Born in Massachusetts on January 17, 1796, Thaddeus Fairbanks moved to St. Johnsbury when he was nineteen years old. St. Johnsbury is in the Northeast Kingdom. Thaddeus set up a wheelwright's shop above his father's gristmill. In 1824, he built an iron foundry with his brother Erastus. The foundry manufactured heating stoves, cast-iron plows and farm implements, which were essential products in rural Vermont. He obtained patents on many of these devices. In 1826, he patented a cast-iron plough that was good for eastern soils.

Four years later, in 1830, the two brothers entered the hemp business with hopes of selling hemp to ropemakers. Thaddeus, a creative, inventive person, patented a hemp and flax dressing machine. However, the business had a major problem with weighing the hemp. This problem would lead to the creation of the products that would make Fairbanks famous. The value of a hemp shipment was based on weight; therefore, hemp needed to be removed from the wagons, weighed and then returned to the wagons. This process was labor intensive, time consuming and costly. However, Thaddeus thought of a clever mechanism that would allow both the hemp and wagon to be easily put on a scale so they could be weighed together. That device would allow the user to deduct the weight of the wagon when it was empty from the wagon's full load of hemp. The resulting number is how much the hemp weighed.

Thaddeus Fairbanks invented the first platform scale, which was patented in 1830. Originally, the brothers thought towns might be interested in using

This artist's rendering of a Fairbanks platform scale shows how fully loaded wagons go on the scale. By deducting the weight of the wagon, it was easy to determine the weight of the load. *Vermont Historical Society, Barre.*

the scales to weigh only hay. However, the market proved to be much greater than weighing hay so, in 1834, Thaddeus and his brothers formed the Fairbanks Scale Company.

The ubiquitous platform scale was to be used around the world for a vast number of different weighing needs at railroads, manufacturing plants, hardware stores, feed shops, physicians' offices, post offices and more. In total, with many improvements, Fairbanks received forty-three patents before he died in St. Johnsbury on April 12, 1886. He is buried in St. Johnsbury, Vermont.

63

OLDEST FLOUR COMPANY

Vermont was not yet a state when, in 1790, Henry Wood, based in Boston, began importing and then distributing flour from England. The fledgling United States had started its first flour company. As the company grew, Wood took on a partner, forming Henry Wood & Company. In the 1820s, after the War of 1812 was fought with Britain, Wood started using American-milled flour.

Ninety years later, in 1870, Benjamin Sands took over the company and renamed it. In 1895, after reorganization, the company was renamed Sands, Taylor and Wood Company (no relation to the original Henry Wood).

In 1896, a new premium brand of flour was introduced. Part owner George Wood had attended a performance of *King Arthur and the Knights of the Roundtable*. This became the inspiration for calling this new high-quality flour "King Arthur" Flour. The new King Arthur product line was a huge success.

In 1917, control of the company went to Frank Sands, son of Orin Sands, who had passed away. The overall market was moving away from retail flour, causing the company to acquire other companies making baking supplies. It gradually introduced new retail products under the name of King Arthur Flour. Later in the 1970s, financial pressures and high interest rates caused the company to sell all but the core flour business.

In 1984, after almost two hundred years in Boston, the company moved from Boston to Norwich, Vermont. The company grew rapidly and, in

1995, initiated a large building campaign that resulted in new facilities, including a baking school and a retail store, which sells a variety of products. In 1996, the company became employee-owned and changed its name to King Arthur Flour. After thirty-five years in Vermont, King Arthur Flour, the first flour company, is still thriving.

64

HEALTHIEST STATE IN THE UNITED STATES

In its 2019 report of America's health rankings, United Health Foundation listed Vermont as first on the list of the healthiest states. The foundation has been ranking states for thirty years, and Vermont is consistently in the top tier. The study is comprehensive, including thirty-five measures in five categories: behaviors, community and environment, policy, clinical care and health outcomes. Some examples of the specific measures are air pollution, violent crimes, drug deaths and frequent mental distress.

Vermont was not number 1 in any of the individual measures. The highest ranking was number 2 for low "violent crime." However, Vermont was first overall. This report is available online.

65

FIRST MONTHLY SOCIAL SECURITY CHECK

Ida May Fuller was born on a farm near Ludlow, Vermont, on September 6, 1874. She attended the Black River Academy in Ludlow, where one of her classmates was Calvin Coolidge. He was two years older but had grown up in nearby Plymouth Notch. At age thirty-one, after working as a schoolteacher, Ida May became a legal secretary.

Ida May filed for her retirement on November 4, 1939, at age sixty-five. When she applied in Rutland, she said she had been paying into "something called Social Security." The Social Security Act had taken effect on August 14, 1935. Since she had been "paying into" the account, she realized she would be eligible to receive benefits. Her first payment into Social Security was for the quarter ending in June 1937, and it was in the amount of $4.50, based on her covered wages of $450. She made a total of $24.75 in payments to Social Security from 1937 to 1939.

Her benefit check, the first monthly check issued by Social Security, was dated January 31, 1940, about three months after she had applied. Although she had paid in a total of $24.75, she received $22,888.92 over her lifespan. She lived to be one hundred years old.

The original intent of Social Security was to give people money to spend, hopefully bringing the country out of the Great Depression. It was not intended to be solely a retirement income stream. Near the end of her life, Ida told a reporter that her Social Security payments "come pretty near paying for my expenses." A frugal Vermonter, Ida May was described as "a kindly, likable, practical and placid woman whose ability to derive deep satisfaction from simple wholesome living has eased her through life."

Ida May Fuller never married. She was born in Vermont, worked in Vermont, died in Vermont at age one hundred and is buried in Vermont. The Social Security Administration has done an excellent job of researching and publishing the history of Ida May Fuller's Social Security payments.

66

LOWEST UNEMPLOYMENT IN UNITED STATES, JULY 2019

The U.S. Bureau of Labor Statistics reported in August 2019 that for July of that year, Vermont's unemployment rate of 2.1 percent was the lowest in the nation. The national average at that time was 3.7 percent. These rankings change month to month and year to year and are subject to adjustment, but Vermont's unemployment has been consistently low. The unemployment rates shown are seasonally adjusted.

67

LAST STATE TO GET A TARGET AND WALMART

Vermonters have always, for the most part, been protective of the environment. In the 1930s, defeating the New Deal's Green Mountain Parkway was a national attention-getter. The state eliminated the scenic eyesores of billboards with 1968 legislation, and Act 250 legislation in 1970 controlled development. Over the years, Vermonters, to varying degrees, have fought the big-box stores.

In 1995, after a five-year court battle, Walmart opened its first store in Vermont. This allowed Walmart to advertise it was located in all fifty states. In 2018, Target, a company that had been in business since 1962, opened its first store in Vermont, and it, too, claimed it was in all fifty states.

There are some similarities in these companies opening in Vermont. Both chains were huge at the time. When Walmart moved into Bennington in 1995, it had about 2,200 U.S. stores, excluding Supercenters. Target, in 2018, had about 1,800 stores before it moved into Burlington.

Forced to go smaller, both companies moved into existing facilities occupied by previous retailers that went out of business. Walmart took over space used by F.W. Woolworth, and Target used previous Bon-Ton space. Both companies used smaller format stores. Walmart's traditional size was 100,000 to 200,000 square feet, but in Bennington, the store was about 50,000. Target's 60,000-square-foot store in Burlington is also smaller than its normal store.

Neither of the big-box stores built stand-alone "boxes," nor were they as "big" as the companies were accustomed to occupying. The Bennington Walmart Superstore was recently completed, after another long struggle, and was expanded to over 110,000 square feet.

Whether being last is good or bad depends on your view. If you never wanted a Walmart or Target, being last means unfortunately they are now here in Vermont. If you had always wanted a Walmart or Target, being last means they are finally here.

68

SHORTEST TIME BEING A "GREAT LAKE"

Vermont's desire to have Lake Champlain formally classified as the sixth "Great Lake" nearly became a permanent reality in 1998. There was a reauthorization of a Sea Grant program that would make certain funds available to Vermont. During this reauthorization process, Senator Patrick Leahy added a few words that formally designated Lake Champlain a Great Lake. Lake Champlain has about five hundred square miles of surface area, but the smallest of the other five lakes, Lake Ontario, has more than seven thousand square miles. However, it has been pointed out that Lake

The steamship *Ticonderoga*, a side paddle wheeler, cruising Lake Champlain in the early 1900s before the lake became a Great Lake. *Library of Congress.*

Champlain's watershed is 18 times the lake area, whereas the Great Lakes watershed is only about 1.2 times the area of the lakes.

President Clinton signed Senate Bill 927 on March 6, 1998, which included the designation of Lake Champlain as a Great Lake. However, there was so much immediate opposition from the states in the Great Lakes region that the Great Lake designation was rescinded eighteen days later on March 24, 1998. For a little over two weeks, Vermont bordered a Great Lake. Fortunately, the eligibility for the funds remained for Lake Champlain.

GENERAL NOTES

AFTERTHOUGHTS

It was not surprising that many of the people associated with these feats were associated with farming. Blacksmithing was also closely associated with farming. Vermont's history is one of small family farms. What was interesting was that many of the people behind these claims to fame had ties to one another. William Hepburn Russell, who started the Pony Express to take mail across the country, was born in Burlington, where Horatio Nelson Jackson, who drove across the United States, made his home. Calvin Coolidge went to the Black River Academy, as did Ida May Fuller, who received the first Social Security check. Paul Harris of Rotary fame also attended Black River. Henry Wells of Wells Fargo was born in Thetford, as were the Camp Fire Girls. Justin Morrill, who gave birth to land grant colleges, went to Thetford Academy. Samuel Read Hall, who started the first school for teachers, and Alexander Twilight, the first African American to receive a college degree, were born in different towns but both ended up in the Northeast Kingdom in Brownington. Two great painters, Norman Rockwell and Grandma Moses, were friends and lived near each other. As you read these stories, other common threads will become apparent.

Claims

There have been some historic claims that are not valid today. According to recent U.S. Census data, Vermont is not the most rural. Maine, according to U.S. Census definitions, is just slightly more rural. U.S. Department of Agriculture figures also indicate Vermont no longer has more milking cows per capita than any other state.

Research

The nature of this book required researching to find if any other group or person was making a similar claim. Therefore, some of the sources listed in the bibliography were used to determine if there were any competing similar claims. Some websites were also used to give leads to other sources. The popular search engines were used in this research effort. Unless specified otherwise, the claims refer to the United States.

Burgoyne's View of Vermonters

Over two hundred years ago, during the founding of Vermont, British general John Burgoyne referred to the settlers who had come to what is now Vermont as the "most active and rebellious race on the continent." (See page 17) Given the large number of claims to fame over the years coming from a state with a historically small population (second-smallest today), Burgoyne's description of Vermonters seemed prophetic.

BIBLIOGRAPHY

Books

Albers, Jan. *Hands on the Land: A History of the Vermont Landscape.* Cambridge, MA: MIT Press, 2000.

Andrews, Edward Deming. *The County Grammar Schools and Academies of Vermont.* Montpelier: Vermont Historical Society, 1936.

Baran, Ed. *Covered Bridges of Vermont.* Woodstock, VT: Countryman Press, 2000.

Bellesiles, Michael A. *Revolutionary Outlaws: Ethan Allen and the Struggle for Independence on the Early American Frontier.* Charlottesville: University Press of Virginia, 1993.

Botham, Noel, and the Useless Information Society. *The Book of Useless Information*: New York: Perigee Group, 2006.

Buckler, Helen, Mary F. Fiedler and Martha F. Allen. *WO-HE-LO, The Story of the Camp Fire Girls 1910–1960.* New York: Holt, Rinehart and Winston, 1961.

Bushnell, Mark. *Hidden History of Vermont.* Charleston, SC: The History Press, 2017

Child, Hamilton. *Gazetteer and Business Directory of Addison County 1881–1882.* Syracuse, NY: Hamilton Child, 1882.

Coffin, Howard. *Something Abides.* Woodstock, VT: Countryman Press, 2013.

Emerson, Jason. *Giant in the Shadows: The Life of Robert Todd Lincoln.* Carbondale: Southern Illinois University Press, 2012.

Farfan, Matthew. *The Vermont-Quebec Border.* Charleston, SC: Arcadia Publishing, 2009.

Federal Writers' Project. *WPA Vermont: A Guide to the Green Mountain State.* 3rd ed. Boston: Houghton Mifflin, 1968.

Fischer, David Hackett. *Paul Revere's Ride.* New York: Oxford University Press, 1994.

Gillies, Paul S. *Law of the Hills: A Judicial History of Vermont.* Barre: Vermont Historical Society, 2019.

Goff, John S. *Robert Todd Lincoln: A Man in His Own Right.* Manchester, VT: Friends of Hildene, 1969.

Hemenway, Abby Maria. *Vermont Historical Gazetteer Volume II.* Burlington, VT: A.M. Hemenway, 1871.

Kane, Joseph Nathan, Steven Anzovin and Janet Podell. *Famous First Facts.* 6th ed. New York: H.W. Wilson Company, 2006.

Kapsch, Robert J. *Canals.* New York: W.W. Norton & Company, 2004.

King, C.J. *Four Marys and a Jessie: The Story of the Lincoln Women.* Manchester, VT: Friends of Hildene, 2015.

Klyza, Christopher McCrory, and Stephen C. Trombulak. *The Story of Vermont: A Natural and Cultural History.* 2nd ed. Lebanon, NH: University Press of New England, 2015.

Knight, Brian L. *No Braver Deeds.* Manchester, VT: Friends of Hildene, 2004.

Labbance, Bob. *The Old Man: The Biography of Walter J. Travis.* Ann Arbor, MI: Sleeping Bear Press, 2000.

Langdon, William Chauncey. *Book of Words: The Pageant of Thetford, Vermont, August 12, 14, 15.* White River Junction: Vermonter Press, 1911.

Lockhart, Betty Ann. *Maple Sugarin' in Vermont.* Charleston, SC: The History Press, 2008.

McFarland, Gerald M. *The Counterfeit Man.* Amherst: University of Massachusetts Press, 1990.

Mello, Robert A. *Moses Robinson and the Founding of Vermont.* Barre: Vermont Historical Society, 2014.

Resch, Tyler. *Dorset: In the Shadow of Marble Mountain.* Dorset, VT: Dorset Historical Society, 1989.

Resnick, Robert J. *Legendary Locals of Burlington.* Charleston, SC: Arcadia Publishing, 2013.

Smith, Richard B. *Ethan Allen and the Capture of Fort Ticonderoga: America's First Victory.* Charleston, SC: The History Press, 2014.

Spurling, Hillary. *Pearl Buck in China.* New York: Simon & Schuster, 2010.

Whitfield, Harvey Amani. *The Problem of Slavery in Early Vermont, 1777–1810.* Barre: Vermont Historical Society, 2014

Wilson, Robert F. *Vermont Curiosities.* Guilford, CT: Morris Book Publishing, 2009.

Articles and Miscellaneous

Adler, Max. "Is the Oldest Club in America Celebrating Its 130th Birthday Today?" *Golf Digest*, September 12, 2016.

Axtell, Dan. "Canal Historic Marker and Other Pictures." danaxtell.com/bf/bfcanal2.html.

Barre Daily Times. "Scouting." November 11, 1910.

Bellis, Mary. "History of the Plow." ThoughtCo., thoughtco.com.

Bentz, Alyssa. "The Real Story Behind the Pony Express." Wells Fargo, www.wellsfargohistory.com/the-real-story-behind-the-pony-express.

Birmingham, Frederick A. "Pearl Buck & The Good Earth of Vermont." *Saturday Evening Post*, Spring 1972.

Black River Academy. "Famous Alumni." bramvt.org.

Bronx Chronicle. "Profile America: Absentee Voting." November 15, 2016.

Buck, Pearl S. "A Dream for Danby." *Yankee Magazine*, July 1971.

———. "My Life on the Mountain." *Ski Magazine*, 1965.

Burns, Ken. *Horatio's Drive: America's First Road Trip*. kenburns.com, 2003.

Bushnell, Mark. "A 1930s Plan Had Vermont Paving Its Peaks." VTDigger, vtdigger.com.

———. "Then Again: Ira Allen's Big Dreams and Big Promises." VTDigger, vtdigger.com.

———. "Then Again: Kipling's Brief and Stormy Stay in Vermont." VTDigger, vtdigger.com.

Celar, Byron N. October 22, 1910 Letter from YMCA to W.F. Milne. Vermont Historical Society, Barre, Vermont.

Colman, Devin. "Dedication of New Historic Marker." VTDigger, vtdigger.com.

Condict, Barbara, and Charles Latham. Thetford Pageant Papers. Thetford Historical Society, thetfordhistoricalsociety.org.

Congress, 112th. S.925 Mt. Andrea Lawrence Designation Act of 2011. congress.gov.

DeWitt, Larry. Details of Ida May Fuller's Payroll Tax Contributions: Research Note #3. U.S. Social Security Administration, July 1996.

Dritschilo, Gordon. "Her Soul Was in Vermont." *Rutland Herald*, October 31, 2018.

Ekwanok Country Club. "Walter Travis (1862–1927) 'The Old Man.'" ekwanok.com.

Estus, Glenn. *Vermont Connection: Vermont as Portrayed on Stamps of the United States*. Westport, NY: Vermont Philatelic Society, 2009.

Federal Highway Administration. *Covered Bridge Manual.* Publication No. FHWA-HRT-04-098, April 2005.

Goldman, Hal. "James Taylor's Progressive Vision: The Green Mountain Parkway." *Vermont History* 63, no. 3 (1995).

Green Mountain Club. "Long Trail." greenmountainclub.org.

Grimes, Kristin. "An Unexpected Marble Quarry Is Hiding Underground in This Mine in Vermont." Only in Your State, onlyinyourstate.com/Vermont.

Guma, Greg. "Boom and Bust in the Quarry Towns." Vermont Way, vermontway.blogspot.com.

Harper, Greg. "Slavery in the North: A Series." Slavery in the North, slavenorth.com.

Homsey, Ed. "Kneeling at the Shrine of the Goddess of Golf." Walter J. Travis Society, travissociety.com.

Jericho Historical Society. "Wilson A. Bentley: The Snowflake Man." Snowflake Bentley, snowflakebentley.com.

Kimball, LeRoy E. "James Wilson of Vermont, America's First Globe Maker." Proceedings of the American Antiquarian Society, 1938.

Lange, Katie. "Medal of Honor Monday: 11 Year-Old Willie Johnston." U.S. Department of Defense, defense.gov.

Marshall, Edward. "Girls Take Up the Boy Scout Idea and Band Together." *New York Times*, March 17, 1912.

Minsinger, W.W. "11-Year-Old Wins Medal of Honor." *Civil War Book of Days* 3, no. 25 (June 2012).

Morrill, Greg. "The Rope Tow." Retro Ski, retro-skiing.com.

———. "Suicide Six: 80 Years of Amazing Firsts." Vermont Mountain Sports and Ride, vtskiandride.com.

Mount Tabor–Danby Historical Society. "Pearl Buck." mtdhistoricalsociety.org/pearl-buck.

National Park Service, Registry of Historic Places and Applications. nps.gov.

Norman Rockwell Museum. "Norman Rockwell and the Boy Scouts of America." nrm.org.

Pendak, Jared. "Couple Acquires Famed Gilberts Hill Property in Woodstock, Pomfret." *Valley News*, January 4, 2017. vnews.com.

Perrin, Noel. "Vermont." In *National Geographic Traveler*, Special Collector's Issue, *50 Destinations of a Lifetime*, October 1999.

Petcare Tips. "Morgan Horse." petcaretips.net/morgan-horse.html.

Podolsky, Mathew. "The Three Musketeers on the Long Trail in 1927." Wild Lens, wildlensinc.org.

Ramsey, Connie Cain. "The Side Judge—A History of Vermont's Assistant Judges." Vermont Association of County Judges, vtassistantjudges.com.

Rotary. "The Education of Paul Harris: From Rascal to Scholar." rotary.org.

Savage, Vance. "The Long Road of Joseph Smith." *Vermont Magazine*, Holiday Issue 2019.

Schiff, Stacy. "The Untold Story of Kipling's American Years." *New York Times*, July 7, 2019.

Sherman, Joshua. "Our State Orchestra." *Stratton Magazine*, Fall 2019.

Silverstein, Hannah. "No Parking: Vermont Rejects the Green Mountain Parkway." *Vermont History* 63, no. 3 (Summer 1995).

Skiver, Kevin. "Winter Olympics 2018: Which States Produce the Most Olympians Per Capita?" CBS Sports, cbssports.com.

Sullivan Museum exhibits, Norwich University, Northfield, Vermont.

Taylor, James P. (1872–1949) Collection 1906–1949, Vermont Historical Society, Barre, Vermont.

Thibault, Amanda. "This Place in History: Fairbanks Scales." My Champlain Valley, mychamplainvalley.com.

———. "This Place in History: First International Hockey Game." My Champlain Valley, mychamplainvalley.com.

United Health Foundation. *America's Health Rankings 30th Edition Annual Report.* United Health Foundation, 2019.

Vane, Sir Francis. British Boy Scout Association letter to William F. Milne dated February 11, 1912. 9 Vincent Square London SW, Grand Scout Master British Division World Scouts.

Vermont Division of Historic Preservation, Historic Markers Montpelier, Vermont. Also accessible accd.vermont.gov/historic-preservation.

Vermont Secretary of State. 1777 Vermont Constitution. Vermont State Archives and Records Administration. Montpelier, Vermont.

Walter, Greg. "The Dancing Master." *Philadelphia Magazine*, July 1969.

Wepman, Dennis Elisha Graves Otis. American National Biography, anb.org.

Williamson, Jeff. "History of: Evolution of Orvis." Outdoor Hub, outdoorhub.com.

Winter, K. "Alexander Twilight (1795–1857)." Black Past, www.blackpast.org.

Woodsmoke Productions and Vermont Historical Society. "Dewey Day: A Century Ends." vermonthistory.org.

Zorachi, Seth M. "Vermont's Tradition of Education and the Vermont Constitution." *Albany Law Review*, April 26, 2006.

Zorn, Marc. "Elisha Otis Inventions and Accomplishments." Vision Launch Media, visionlaunch.com.

Websites

American Legislative Exchange Council, alec.org.
American Morgan Horse Association, morganhorse.com.
America's Health Rankings, americashealthrankings.org.
Ancestry, ancestry.com.
Barre Montpelier Times Argus, timesargus.com.
Bennington Museum, benningtonmuseum.org.
Biography, biography.com
Black America, blackamericaweb.com.
Charterhouse of the Transfiguration, transfiguration.chartreux.org.
Civil War, civilwar.com.
Company Histories, company-histories.com.
Dorset Field Club, dorsetfieldclub.com.
Dorset Historical Society, dorsetvthistory.org.
Edison Nation, blog.edisonnation.com/category/learning-from-inventors.
Encyclopedia Britannica, britannica.com.
Encyclopedia of American Politics, ballotpedia.org.
Find a Grave, findagrave.com.
The Free Library, thefreelibrary.com.
Free Online Encyclopedia, encyclopedia.com.
Greg Guma, muckraker-gg.blogspot.com.
Heads Up. "Norman Rockwell." headsup.boyslife.org.
Historical Marker Database, hmdb.org.
Historic Elmwood Cemetery and Foundation, elmwoodhistoriccemetery.org.
History Channel, history.com.
Home of the American Civil War, civilwarhome.com.
Improve Dyslexia, improvedyslexia.com.
International Skiing History Association, skiinghistory.org.
John Deere, johndeere.com
The Junto, earlyamericanists.com.
Justin Smith Morrill, morrillhomestead.org.
King Arthur Flour, kingarthurflour.com.
Landmark College, landmark.edu.
Library of Congress, loc.gov.
Merriam-Webster, merriam-webster.com.
Morgan Horse Heritage Foundation, morganhorseheritagefoundation.com.
Mount Equinox, Vermont, equinoxmountain.com.
National Agricultural Statistics Service, nass.usda.gov.

National Museum of American History, americanhistory.si.edu.
National Pony Express Association, nationalponyexpress.org.
New England Historical Society, newenglandhistoricalsociety.com.
Northern Vermont University, northernvermont.edu.
Northwestern Pritzker School of Law, law.northwestern.edu.
Norwich University, norwich.edu.
Obscure Vermont, obscurevermont.com.
Oldest, oldest.org.
Old Stone House Museum, oldstonehousemuseum.org.
One World Globes, 1worldglobes.com.
On This Day, onthisday.com.
Orvis, orvis.com.
Outdoor Advertising Association of America, oaaa.org.
Records Finder, recordsfinder.com.
Rotary International, rotary.org.
Scenic America, scenic.org.
Seven Days, sevendaysvt.com.
Snowflake Bentley, snowflakebentley.com.
Social Security Administration, ssa.gov.
Sports Illustrated, si.com.
U.S. Bureau of Labor Statistics, bls.gov.
U.S. Census, census.gov.
U.S. Customs and Border Protection, cbp.gov.
U.S. Department of Agriculture, usda.gov.
U.S. Military, usmilitary.com.
Vermont Academy, vermontacademy.org.
Vermont Dairy Industry Association, vdia.org.
Vermont General Assembly, legislature.vermont.gov.
Vermont Historical Society, vermonthistory.org.
Vermont Maple Syrup Makers, vermontmaple.org.
Vermont Marble Museum, vermontmarblemuseum.org.
Vermont Philatelic Society, vermontps.org.
Vermont Quarries Corporation, vermontquarries.com.
Vermont Sports Hall of Fame, vermontsportshall.com.
Vermont State Historic Sites, historicsites.vermont.gov.
Vermont Symphony Orchestra, vso.org.
The Vermont Way, vermontway.blogspot.com.
VTDigger, vtdigger.com.
Walter J. Travis Society, travissociety.org.

Wikimedia Commons, commons.wikimedia.org.
Wikipedia, wikipedia.org.
Wild Lens, wildlensinc.org.
Wisconsin Online, wisconline.com.

INDEX

O

P

R

S

T

V

W

Y

ABOUT THE AUTHOR

Throughout his corporate career, Dick Smith has been interested in history. Dick has created historical maps and self-guided tours of Vermont that have been published and distributed throughout the Northeast. Both of Dick's previous books, *The Revolutionary War in Bennington County: A History and Guide* and *Ethan Allen and the Capture of Fort Ticonderoga: America's First Victory*, have been on bestseller lists and recommended by Vermont Public Radio (VPR). He has appeared on VPR's radio show *Vermont Edition*. A past president of the Manchester Historical Society, Dick is currently serving his third three-year term as a trustee of the Vermont Historical Society. For over twenty years, he has been giving history tours and has appeared on WCAX TV (CBS) for these tours. Acting as host, his award-winning public television history series, *History Where It Happened*, was filmed throughout Vermont. He has made presentations in New England and New York.

He earned degrees in engineering and management from Lehigh University and an advanced degree in economics from Columbia University. He resides in Manchester, Vermont, with his wife, Sharon.